Roy Wilkins:
Leader
of the NAACP

Roy Wilkins:
Leader
of the NAACP

Calvin Craig Miller

620 South Elm Street, Suite 223
Greensboro, North Carolina   27406
http://www.morganreynolds.com

ROY WILKINS: LEADER OF THE NAACP

Library of Congress Cataloging-in-Publication Data

Miller, Calvin Craig, 1954-
  Roy Wilkins : leader of the NAACP / Calvin Craig Miller.
    p. cm.
Includes bibliographical references and index.
  ISBN 13: 978-1-931798-49-5
  ISBN 10: 1-931798-49-4
1. Wilkins, Roy, 1901—Juvenile literature. 2. African
Americans—Biography—Juvenile literature. 3. Civil rights workers—United
States—Biography—Juvenile literature. 4. National Association for the
Advancement of Colored People—Juvenile literature. 5. African
Americans—Civil rights—History—20th century—Juvenile literature. I. Title.
  E185.97.W69M55 2005
  323'.092—dc22

2004027688

Printed in the United States of America
First Edition

Contents

Roy Wilkins in 1970. *(AP Photo)*

One

From Poverty to Prosperity

Whittier Grammar School was a pleasant brick building just a few blocks from Roy Wilkins's new home on Galtier Street, a quiet, leafy street in St. Paul, Minnesota. In the fall of 1907, six-year-old Roy had arrived from St. Louis, Missouri, to live with his Aunt Elizabeth and Uncle Sam. On the first day of school, Aunt Elizabeth walked with him to the door, and then the principal brought him to his new classroom. Roy was already finding Minnesota to be very different from Missouri. Still, it was a tremendous surprise for him to look around the room and realize that every single one of his new classmates had white skin. He had come a long way from the segregated kindergarten he had attended in the Jim Crow South.

Years later, writing in his autobiography, Wilkins

St. Paul, Minnesota, was a growing city when Roy came there to live in the early 1900s. *(Library of Congress)*

would look back on his days at Whittier Grammar School fondly. Though he looked different from the other students in his class, no one made a big deal about the color of his skin. The same was true of the working-class neighborhood Elizabeth and Sam Williams called home. In the early 1900s, Roy's new surroundings were full of hard-working, immigrant families, mainly from Europe.

"Everyone around us, white and Negro alike, was struggling to support a middle-class outlook on a poor man's income," he later recalled. "Hard work, thrift, education for the children, a sense of pride in home and country, faith in the future—those were the ruling values up and down Galtier Street." Roy's experience growing up in an integrated neighborhood in the Midwest gave him a unique perspective on what the thinker W. E. B. Du

Bois called the problem of the twentieth century: the problem of the color line.

As he grew up and became a vital contributor to the fight for freedom for all Americans, Roy Wilkins would always return to the lessons he learned as a child in Minnesota. The sea of white faces from his first day of grammar school quickly became Roy's friends, reinforcing his belief that racism was something learned, that children did not see color the way adults did. His happy days on Galtier Street engraved into Roy's heart and mind a conviction that all Americans could find a way to live together: "No one can tell me that it is impossible for white people and black people to live

Roy with a group of his high school friends, with whom he formed a bicycle club. *(Library of Congress)*

next door to one another, to get along—even to love one another. For me integration is not an abstraction constructed on dusty eighteenth-century notions of democracy. I believe in it not only because it is right but because I have lived it all my life." This belief would be tested, time and again, by blacks and whites alike, but Roy Wilkins never gave up the faith his upbringing had given him.

Roy's father, William Wilkins, had a different perspective. Born in Holly Springs, Mississippi, in 1878, just fifteen years after President Abraham Lincoln issued the Emancipation Proclamation that freed the slaves of the South, William grew up dirt poor. His father, Asberry Wilkins, was a sharecropper whose former owner gave him some land, a mule, and farming supplies so Asberry could work long hours in the field and "share" half the profits from his crops. The family had very little money—even their last name was borrowed from a white man.

William Wilkins managed to gain some education, attending Rust College, an institution administered by the African Methodist Church. He became one of the first Wilkinses to achieve literacy. In 1900, he met and married a local schoolteacher, Mayfield Edmundson, called Sweetie by her friends. A very dangerous force soon threatened the young couple's new life: William Wilkins's temper.

After the Civil War, the South entered a period called Reconstruction. Overseen by federal troops and hugely unpopular with wealthy white farmers, Reconstruction was designed to restore order to a land ravaged by war. It was also geared toward helping freed slaves find employment and education. For a time, great strides were made as blacks were elected to office, offered free education, and able to open their own businesses. But a combination of factors, including corruption, pressure from formerly powerful white farmers, and the problems of the presidential election of 1876, brought Reconstruction to an end just over ten years after it had begun. Power quickly returned to those who had held it before the war, and the backlash against African Americans was severe.

By the turn of the century, the South had passed a number of what would come to be known as Jim Crow laws, named after a popular minstrel show character that portrayed derogatory stereotypes of African Americans. These laws varied from town to town and state to state, but all had one goal in mind: to restrict the freedoms of black citizens. Poll taxes (levied on blacks, not whites) and so-called literacy tests (often consisting of obscure questions and given only to black voters) effectively disenfranchised black voters. Other laws limited their social freedoms: blacks and whites could not date or marry or even occupy the same railroad car. Black people could be arrested for using a public library, for entering a public toilet, or even for being out after dark in some towns. Violence against African Americans swept the South, either implicitly or openly condoned by local authorities.

In this highly charged environment, deep in one of the states most infamous for abusing African Americans, William Wilkins committed an unthinkable act: he beat a white man unconscious.

It happened one day in June of 1900, when William was walking in the road and heard someone yell from behind him, "Nigger, get out of my way." Instead of stepping to the side, William jumped onto the man's wagon and punched him in the face. Roger Wilkins, William's grandson, later summed up the situation: "My grandfather had whipped a white man who'd been discourteous to him, and you didn't do that in Holly Springs, Mississippi, and live to tell about it."

By evening, word of William's act had spread across the county. Everyone knew William and Sweetie had to get out of town as fast as they could. They packed their things quickly and got on the next train headed to St. Louis, Missouri. Roger Wilkins said his grandfather "ran north just ahead of a lynch mob that was out to kill him."

William carried a piece of paper bearing the address of a friend who had also moved to St. Louis. He and Sweetie stayed with that family while he searched for a job. William scrounged for any work he could get, finally getting hired at a brick kiln on the east side of town. Their son Roy was born about a year later on August 30, 1901. The Wilkinses counted their first-born child lucky not to have lived a day near the old plantations of Holly Springs.

Despite the relative safety of St. Louis compared to Holly Springs, the Wilkins family made their home on Laclede Avenue in an all-black area of town. Roy lived in St. Louis for the first five years of his life, hardly ever seeing white faces. A growing family stretched his father's thin wages. Roy gained a sister, Armeda, in 1903, and a brother, Earl, in 1905. Roy and his siblings played happily together, raising a joyful racket in the small row house on Laclede Avenue. But they learned quickly to lower their voices when their father came home. William's temper heated quickly and he was full of bitterness at his lot in life.

Roy was sometimes puzzled by his father's rage. William came home dusty and tired, frowning from weariness and resentment, looking like a beaten-down man even to his young son. William began to seek solace

The house where Roy was born in St. Louis, Missouri. *(Library of Congress)*

in the Bible, reading long passages out loud at the dinner table while Roy fidgeted and the food cooled. Roy did not much care for the long dinnertime Bible lessons, and even less for church, but he admired his father's conviction that racism was wrong. "I have the same traits buried somewhere in my chromosomes," Roy wrote in his autobiography. "I don't like to be mistreated. I don't like to see other people mistreated. I believe in fighting back."

Even as a little boy, Roy was an introvert. He had few close friends outside his brother and sister, and he spent long hours alone. He was happy that way, but he would eventually learn that his silence made him seem distant to those around him.

Roy *(right)* with his sister, Armeda, and brother, Earl. *(Library of Congress)*

The same year Roy entered kindergarten at the Banneker School, his mother was diagnosed with tuberculosis. At the time, there was no cure and no vaccine; it was a death sentence. Sweetie Wilkins immediately wrote a desperate letter to her sister Elizabeth, who lived in St. Paul, Minnesota. She was afraid that William would have to send their children to their grandparents and begged Elizabeth to take them instead. She did not want her children to grow up in the South.

Sweetie died just a short time after writing that letter. Two days later, a robust, vigorous, light-skinned woman arrived at Laclede Avenue. It was Aunt Elizabeth. She quickly took charge of the family's affairs, even arranging for her sister's funeral. Though she could see that William was not capable of caring for three small children, Elizabeth planned to take only the youngest one, Earl, home with her. But Elizabeth's husband, Sam, insisted she bring all three. So as soon as Sweetie was buried, Roy, Armeda, and Earl said goodbye to their father and boarded a train north.

Roy Wilkins's aunt, Elizabeth Williams.

Their new home on Galtier Street was unlike anything they had ever seen before. Sam and Elizabeth Williams worked hard to make a comfort-

found William a job as a fireman at a local fire station, quite a respectable position in the community. Then William announced that he wanted to reclaim his children. Elizabeth asked what his plans for them were. William said he might take the family back to Mississippi. Elizabeth could hardly believe her ears.

Sam and Elizabeth immediately engaged an attorney and won legal custody of the Wilkins children. Roy, Armeda, and Earl would not be taken back to the South.

Two

Birth of the NAACP

The early 1900s saw a tremendous migration of African Americans out of the South into the North and West. They left to try to find better economic and social opportunities for themselves and their families. But moving was not easy. Discrimination was present outside of the South, and for the majority of blacks who lacked a good education, low-paying jobs were low-paying jobs no matter where they were found.

One of the period's great black leaders urged his people to stay in the South. "Cast down your buckets where you are," Booker T. Washington said at an exposition in Atlanta in 1895. In what came to be known as the Atlanta Compromise speech, Washington told a predominately white audience, "it is in the South that the Negro is given a man's chance in the commercial world."

The faculty and staff of the Tuskegee Institute in 1906. *From left to right, seated in the front row:* R. C. Ogden, Margaret Murray Washington, Booker T. Washington, Andrew Carnegie, and an unidentified person.

Washington had gained renown as the director of Alabama's Tuskegee Institute, which opened in 1881 with the goal of teaching such skills as farming, crafts, and trades to free blacks. Washington believed that hard work would lead to economic success for African Americans, which would then lead to social and political equality. He counseled his followers not to agitate for immediate freedom but to endure their privations until they could earn those freedoms. Washington's conciliatory stance made him a favorite of white leaders and the Tuskegee Institute boasted excellent funding. But not everyone agreed with his plans.

Along with William Shakespeare, Geoffrey Chaucer, and Robert Burns, one of the writers Roy read in school was W. E. B. Du Bois. Though Roy felt no direct relationship to the world Du Bois described, he was intrigued by the way Du Bois wrote about black people.

William Edward Burghardt Du Bois was an African American born in Great Barrington, Massachusetts, into a family that had been free for at least one hundred years. A dapper man with a neatly trimmed goatee, Du Bois earned a PhD from Harvard in 1895. He taught at Atlanta University, where he helped guide a generation of young black students to the rewards of higher education.

W. E. B. Du Bois. *(Courtesy of Art Resource.)*

Du Bois, in contrast to Booker T. Washington, believed education was the only route to an African-American cultural revolution, one he insisted would be led by the black intellectual elite. He called them the "Talented Tenth."

"The Negro race, like all races, is going to saved by its exceptional men," Du Bois wrote. "The problem of education among Negroes must first of all deal with the Talented Tenth; it is the problem of developing the Best of this race that they may guide the Mass away from the contamination and death of the Worst in their own and other races." Du Bois also advocated for immediate economic, social, and political equality for all people of color. He could not see why anyone would not want to claim the rights guaranteed to them by the federal government but denied because of racism.

Roy was an excellent student, soaking up all the books and articles he could get his hands on. As he progressed through school, his teachers remarked on the promise his writing showed and encouraged him to pursue it. Roy began winning composition contests, proudly showing off his certificates to his beaming foster parents. Elizabeth and Sam supported Roy in everything he did, showing him through their example that hard work and dignity made most things possible.

Growing up in an integrated middle-class neighborhood in Minnesota, Roy had been spared the many cruelties of Jim Crow laws. It would be some time, in fact, before he realized that racial injustice existed outside of the South. When Roy was ten, an organization was formed to combat the rise of violence and oppression against African Americans. It would be the organization that would become the foundation for most of Roy's adult life.

In the summer of 1908, a mob lynched a black barber in Springfield, Illinois, the birthplace of Abraham Lincoln. The next night an African-American man was killed because he was married—and had been for more than twenty years—to a white woman. Thousands of black Americans fled for their lives and the governor had to call out the state militia to quell the violence.

The next year, on February 12, 1909, sixty people, including W. E. B. Du Bois, signed the founding document of what would become the National Association for the Advancement of Colored People (NAACP). Most of the founders were wealthy white activists who resented the injustice perpetrated against African Americans. They asked W. E. B. Du Bois and others to join them in forming an organization to protest racism and discrimination. The association hired African-American attorneys and other professionals to force changes to laws designed to oppress black Americans and to see that the courts enforced equal rights.

Roy practically grew up with the NAACP, for his family was linked to it from the beginning. One of his aunt and uncle's friends was the attorney Frederick L. McGhee—the same lawyer who had helped Sam and Elizabeth win custody of the Wilkins children. McGhee founded the Twin Cities Protective League, a group he had hoped to affiliate with the NAACP. But McGhee died shortly after founding the league, and the organization dissolved. W. E. B. Du Bois came to St. Paul in 1913 seeking to revive McGhee's efforts. St. Paul residents responded by organizing an NAACP branch, and Roy's uncle Sam became one of its first members. As he grew up, Roy read about racial issues in copies of *The Crisis,* the magazine Du Bois edited for the NAACP, as they arrived in the mail.

World War I began in Europe in 1914. Though President Wilson initially tried to keep America neutral in the conflict, German submarines, called U-boats, targeted passenger ships crossing the Atlantic, killing Americans in the process. By the spring of 1917, Wilson felt he had no choice but to ask Congress for a declaration of war, in order, as he said, to keep the world safe for democracy.

Thousands of young black men seized on the opportunity offered by the war to prove their patriotism. They enlisted in droves—almost 400,000 black soldiers served. Despite their willingness to fight, most African Americans were relegated to menial tasks, and all of them served in segregated units, usually distinguished by a lack of equipment and poor training. It took public protests from black leaders before the government would allow any black officers to be commissioned, and when they finally were, they were not allowed to command white troops. A few units of black soldiers, among them the famed Harlem Hellfighters, did see combat action in

Meuse-Argonne, September 26-October 1, 1918. Despite heavy casualties, the 369th Infantry, called the Harlem Hellfighters, fought valiantly in the Allied offensive as part of the French 161st Division. Attacking behind a fiery barrage, the 369th Infantry assaulted successive German trench lines and captured the town of Ripont.

France. They fought bravely and well, and were much appreciated by the French people. Members of the Hellfighters, who spent more than six months in combat, were the first Americans to receive the French Croix de Guerre for bravery.

When the war ended in 1918, black soldiers returned home buoyed by their success overseas. They found a country in the midst of an economic boom sparked by the defense industry. Though many of those jobs were not available to black workers, thousands of African Americans streamed north to escape Jim Crow and to find better jobs. This migration from the rural South into the cities of the North had a tremendous impact on American society. In the years to come, New York City in particular would become a vibrant center for African-American culture and art, a period known as the Harlem Renaissance.

But there was a darker shadow that moved up out of the South at the same time—the specter of racism. Decorated soldiers who happened to be African Americans were beaten for Jim Crow offenses—while wearing their uniforms. The summer Roy Wilkins turned eighteen was marked by a series of race riots across the country. Seventy African Americans were lynched during what became known as the Red Summer. The violence did more to reveal the ugliness of racial hatred than any of Du Bois's impassioned editorials could, but from the shelter of Roy's quiet, integrated neighborhood in St. Paul, these conflicts seemed like remote events, not a part of life in the ethnic melting pot of Minnesota. But in June of 1920, the John Robinson Circus arrived in Duluth. Before the circus folded its tents to leave town, a violent mob would write an ugly chapter in Minnesota history.

On the night of June 14, two Duluth teenagers, Irene Tusken and James Sullivan, went to the circus. For reasons still unclear

An advertisement for the John Robinson Circus.

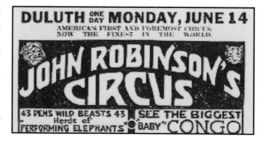

today, James Sullivan told his father later that night that he had been held at gunpoint while three black laborers for the circus raped Tusken. Tusken corroborated his story, though a physical examination showed no evidence she had been assaulted. There were no other witnesses to the alleged crime, but six African-American men were immediately arrested.

As word spread through town the next day, fueled by a newspaper headline screaming "WEST DULUTH GIRL VICTIM OF SIX NEGROES," a crowd estimated at between a thousand and ten thousand people gathered outside the Duluth city jail at Second Avenue and Superior Street. On the night of the fifteenth, the mob became violent, storming the jail and overpowering the police. All six arrested men were broken out

WEST DULUTH GIRL VICTIM OF SIX NEGROES

Attacked on Circus Grounds While Watching Load-

Headline in the *Duluth Herald*, June 15, 1920.

of their cells. The mob lynched Elias Clayton, Elmer Jackson, and Isaac McGhie, leaving their bodies hanging from city lampposts. The Minnesota National Guard arrived the next morning in time to save the three surviving black prisoners, moving them to the St. Louis County jail.

Newspapers around the country carried the story. The *Minneapolis Journal* wrote that the lynch mob had put

This photograph of the Duluth lynching victims was taken shortly after they had been beaten and hanged by the mob.

"an effaceable stain on the name of Minnesota," and added, "The sudden flaming up of racial passion, which is the reproach of the South, may also occur, as we now learn in the bitterness of humiliation, in Minnesota."

Roy Wilkins had heard all his life that he was beyond the reach of racist violence and murder. Now, at nineteen, the Duluth episode brought home the understanding that race could cost people their lives anywhere in America. He later wrote that he felt "sick, scared and angry all at the same time."

Roy enrolled at the University of Minnesota that fall and wrote an award-winning essay on the lynchings, declaring the murders a threat to democracy. Years of reading Du Bois's calls to action in the pages of *The Crisis* had moved Roy in an abstract way. The Duluth lynchings made his hatred for injustice the defining aspect of his life. As he later wrote, "For the first time in my life I understood what Du Bois had been writing about. I found myself thinking of black people as a very vulnerable *us*—and white people as an unpredictable, violent *them.*"

Three

Newspaper Crusader

Roy continued his academic success at the University of Minnesota. He excelled at writing and won a cash prize for a speech he gave about the murders in Duluth. The money went toward his tuition, as did the money he earned in a variety of summer jobs. He caddied at a golf course, worked in a slaughterhouse, and served as a porter on a railroad car—a job his uncle Sam helped him get. Living at home helped him save some money, but no matter how much a nickel meant, Roy was not afraid to reject one on principle. The summer he worked on the railroad, Roy was given a nickel tip he considered insultingly small for his service. He looked at the woman, then at the nickel in his hand, and threw the change out the window.

Roy stood up for himself while in college, too. When

Wilkins worked as a waiter on trains in the Great Lakes region during his summer vacations from college. Here he is posed outside one of the dining cars. *(Library of Congress)*

he discovered black students could not join the campus fraternities, he founded one they could. Though he was active on campus, he was not considered a true leader, mainly because he still preferred time alone to read and think. His distant nature made him seem aloof to some that did not know him well, something Roy regretted. Still, he was more comfortable at his desk than in a crowd. He found his niche as a reporter for the campus paper.

The *Minnesota Daily* had not had a black reporter until Wilkins came along. He began at the bottom, like any new reporter, covering small events and writing brief stories. Soon he was getting more of his writing in the paper, writing about subjects that interested him and discovering the power of the press.

Wilkins quickly realized that newspaper reporting fit his personality. He had grown into a tall young man with a deep voice, plainspoken in the midwestern manner, with penetrating eyes that appeared thoughtful as he listened during interviews. True to his upbringing in St. Paul, he wanted to believe the best about people. But with his birth father's disposition, he tended to let racial injustice simmer and fill him with a rage that constantly threatened to spill over. He learned that newspaper writers did not have to use their fists to express their anger, however. The front page and editorial columns allowed him to vent his rage at racism without the kind of physical assault that had driven William Wilkins's family out of Mississippi.

Black newspapers of the time stood alone as outlets for in-depth reporting about lynchings and race riots. Most white newspapers either blamed such events on blacks or buried them in small back-page articles. Their

The University of Minnesota in the early 1920s. *(Library of Congress)*

editors marginalized the black population in many ways, often by refusing to print photographs of African Americans in their pages. Papers run by African Americans were usually the only sources for race news, including the truth about violence against blacks. For their human-interest sections, black editors ran major features on black entertainers and artists, and emphasized the achievements of black schools and colleges. Because they dared to publish the truth, black journalists flirted with danger.

Those journalists who braved the threat of violence to themselves or their families were following in the tradition of journalism inspired by the Progressive movement. Born in response to the privations of the poor and working-class people—packed into cities by turn-of-the-century industrialism—the Progressive movement emphasized care for humanity and belief in the dignity of the individual. Middle- and upper-class people like Jane Addams of Chicago's Hull House lobbied cities to provide basic services like sanitation and education to their poorer residents. Progressives understood the power of the press to sway public opinion yet believed that journalists had a responsibility not to sensationalize. They founded schools to teach journalists how to present the facts of a situation as objectively as possible, setting the bar for the style of journalism still used today.

Roy loved his work on the *Daily*. He would stay up through the night and into the early morning, laying out the front page and proofreading the copy. The work was demanding and he did not earn much money, but Roy enjoyed it. Unfortunately, the *Daily* was in financial trouble. It had barely enough subscribers to keep afloat. Staffers mounted subscription drives but they could not attract enough new readers to pay the paper's bills. They finally had to cut costs by reducing the size of the newspaper to a pamphlet. Roy wanted to be a newspaperman, not a pamphleteer.

He soon got his chance to work on a bigger paper when a friend, Walter Chestnutt, founded a weekly called the *Northwestern Bulletin.* Roy helped him edit the fledgling paper. His writing for the *Bulletin* attracted the attention of other editors in St. Paul. When the editor of the *St. Paul Appeal* was killed in an accident, his widow offered Roy a job. Roy, then twenty-one, jumped at the chance to take over a bigger paper. He had recently become a member of the St. Paul chapter of the NAACP so he had a keen interest in the presentation of issues important to African Americans. Editing his own paper would give him a chance to exert some control over news relevant to his people.

When Roy took over the paper in December of 1922, the *Appeal* was in a sorry state. Roy wanted a new look, more news stories instead of soft features, and a sharper, more relevant editorial tone. He stopped the paper's practice of selling ads for the front page and got rid of the stories he considered fluff. He ran editorial and news stories on racial issues, lynchings, and the Ku Klux Klan.

Many of Roy's beliefs about what a paper should do

Du Bois, far right, in the NAACP offices of *The Crisis. (Library of Congress)*

came from *The Crisis,* the magazine W. E. B. Du Bois
edited for the NAACP. It was in those pages that he read
of Du Bois's belief in Pan-Africanism, a philosophy that
urged political union between African Americans and
African nations. By the turn of the century, most of
Africa had been divided up and taken as colonies by
various European nations. These colonies existed to
benefit their "parent" nations, and as a result the people
who lived in them were often abused and exploited.
Having studied the writings of Karl Marx while pursuing
graduate work in Germany, Du Bois was convinced that
economic inequity was at the root of all inequality. He
saw the struggle against racism in economic terms, and
he was particularly struck by the economic oppression
experienced by Africans in their native countries.

Du Bois's focus on African problems exasperated Wilkins. The continued virulence of American racism convinced him that African Americans could not be diverted from the march toward justice in their own country. Black Americans could be hanged without trial, denied their right to vote, and walled outside the mainstream of society for their entire lives. How could Du Bois insist that blacks in the United States spend their time and energy on African concerns?

"Du Bois acknowledges that 'Pan-Africa' is a dream," Roy wrote. "And so it is. But lynching, disenfranchisement, segregation and a thousand and one evils are not dreams. They are terrible realities. Du Bois should cut out his wild dreams and use his time and talents in fighting the awful things that be."

Wilkins's passion for his subject showed, and though he would later regret his harsh criticism of Du Bois, he was making a name and a career for himself. Both his talent and a bit of luck helped him take another step up in 1923, shortly after he graduated from the University of Minnesota.

His father, William, had finally found his niche, living in Missouri and becoming a successful preacher in the African-American Methodist church. His church bulletins were printed in a Kansas City shop owned by Chester Arthur Franklin, who also published the *Kansas City Call*. One day Franklin mentioned that he needed a news editor. Excited by the chance to help a son others had raised, William told Franklin that Roy was a journalist and would be just the man for the job.

Franklin wrote Roy about the opening. Wilkins jumped at the chance to move to a bigger paper for better pay. He was offered a test assignment: he could cover the weeklong meeting of the NAACP. If Franklin liked his stories, Roy would get the job. The assignment was a natural.

The NAACP was meeting in Kansas City in an effort to raise awareness about its activism. The association had been trying for several years to bring attention to the problem of lynching and related racial violence in America. In 1921, Missouri congressman L. C. Dyer had introduced an anti-lynching bill that would not merely investigate lynchings, as some in Congress advocated, but hold states liable for failure to prevent them. The association threw all of its weight behind the Dyer bill. It passed the U.S. House of Representatives in a raucous session that sparked angry shouts between African-American spectators in the gallery and Southern lawmakers, only to be defeated in the Senate.

Despite the achievements of black Americans, the glories of the Harlem Renaissance, and even the brave volunteer service African-American soldiers rendered in the war, the bottom line was that race relations were not getting better. And people were in disagreement over how to change that.

At the Kansas City meeting, a representative of Missouri governor Arthur M. Hyde told the audience that black Americans should simply work harder, rather than attempting to pursue so lofty a goal as equality with whites. The crowd almost shouted him down, but an association leader persuaded them to let him finish. When he did, NAACP secretary James Weldon Johnson rose to reply. He told the governor's man that hard work had gotten African Americans nowhere.

"Look around you, sir, at these thousands who by thrift and industry, by study and by devotion to the church, have made themselves worthy to enjoy the rights of American citizens," he said. "But sir, do they enjoy them?" The crowd's thunderous applause provided the obvious answer to Johnson's cynical question. Wilkins seized on it as a perfect ending to his story.

Wilkins's coverage of the NAACP's convention earned him a job. Franklin offered him $100 a month, a solid salary in those days. Wilkins packed his bags, said good-bye to the relatives who had sustained him throughout his childhood in St. Paul, and embarked on what would become an eight-year-long career as a Kansas City newspaperman.

Four

Return to the South

In 1923, the Harlem Renaissance was in full swing. Black writers, artists, musicians, and intellectuals had created a vibrant and exciting community in New York City, drawing white and black patrons alike to night-clubs, bookstores, and art shows. The renaissance was also having a ripple effect across the country, spreading its message of pride in black culture and achievement. But outside of the urban centers of the North, things were changing much more slowly.

In Kansas City, Missouri, four hundred miles south of St. Paul, Roy Wilkins encountered a city divided. The *Kansas City Call* was a leading weekly for African Americans, and Kansas City had many important and successful black citizens. But there was also an element of racism unlike any Wilkins had seen before, one which he would soon come to experience firsthand and bitterly resent.

Though taking the job meant leaving the only home he had ever really known, Wilkins was thrilled at the opportunity to be a part of a thriving newspaper. Chester Arthur Franklin had scrounged the money to start the paper just a few years before and, through hard work, had built it into a small but respected weekly.

Wilkins soon came to know and admire Franklin's determination and integrity. He learned that his boss had purchased his own printing press so as not to rely on white-owned typesetting businesses, only to find that the printers' union had refused to allow any of its members to teach him how to use it. The machine sat in the office for half a year before Franklin was able to puzzle it out.

The main white paper in town was the *Kansas City Star*. Wilkins came to dislike that paper intensely, as it

The intersection of 15th and Holmes, a popular nightlife area in Kansas City in 1920. *(Library of Congress)*

refused to publish pictures of African Americans and relegated any racially related news to the back page (if it was printed at all). But he was too savvy to pass up a learning opportunity and would not hesitate to query *Star* reporters about breaking stories. Franklin liked the young

Chester Arthur Franklin, founder of the *Call*. *(Library of Congress)*

man and gave him the opportunity to bring political and social articles to the fore. He eventually gave Wilkins his own column, "Talking It Over," in which Roy was able to discuss stories about prejudice in Kansas City, the absurdity of Jim Crow laws, and the problems caused by segregated housing. When people claimed blacks had opportunities they really did not possess, Wilkins was there to set the record straight. One of his favorite things to do in his column was to turn racial stereotypes on their heads. He delighted in reports of white people committing crimes unfairly associated with African Americans, trying as always to show that the differences between the races were far smaller than people might otherwise believe.

As much as Wilkins appreciated his new position and the power it offered him to reach out to his readers, it still rankled him that Kansas City was not the pleasant, integrated community he had grown up in. Years later, Wilkins could still remember vividly the smallest details of his own experiences with discrimination. Once, Wilkins offered his seat on a trolley to an older white woman. As he later wrote, "She eyed me frostily, turned her back on the seat, and snapped to a white man standing next to her, 'I'm not old enough yet to accept a seat from a nigger.'" Incidents like this struck Wilkins to the core and convinced him that the people of Kansas City suffered from the same delusions about African Americans that had been in place for centuries.

Even before Abraham Lincoln's Emancipation Proclamation freed the slaves of the South, people had been divided about the best way to create a just and equal society for all citizens. In the early years of the twentieth century, a number of organizations arose to try to bring attention to the rampant discrimination against African Americans. Two of the most important—both still in existence today—were the NAACP and the National Urban League.

The National Urban League was founded just one year after the NAACP, in 1910. It shared many of the same goals as the NAACP, though it put more emphasis on ensuring adequate social services for those economically disadvantaged and, as its name suggests, focused much of its effort in urban centers. Both organizations made use of the court system to try to ensure that laws already in place guaranteeing social and political equality were enforced. The NAACP advocated the use of nonviolent protest to resist discriminatory practices and institutions, and held rallies and sent orators across the country to raise awareness and interest in the fight for equal rights. The NAACP also maintained a strong public presence, showing the strength possible in numbers. By holding its 1920 annual meeting in Atlanta, Georgia, considered by many to be a bastion of the Ku Klux Klan, the NAACP made a clear statement that it would not be intimidated. The NAACP and other groups like the Urban League offered people hope and inspiration.

Roy became a more active member of the NAACP during his years in Kansas City. He eventually took a leadership position with the Kansas City chapter, serving as its secretary. Between that and the paper, his time was well filled. Still, just as the lynchings in Duluth had a strong impact on the teenage Wilkins, so did another similar injustice stir Roy to further commit himself to activism.

In September of 1925, an African-American doctor named Ossian Sweet bought a house in a white Detroit neighborhood. Though Detroit had a sizable black population, most of those people lived in a run-down area called Black Bottom. Sweet wanted something better for his wife and daughter. Oddly, the woman who sold Sweet the house had been married to black man, but his skin was so light their neighbors either chose to ignore it or

The Sweet home at 2905 Garland in Detroit in 1926.

never realized their community was already integrated. However, once word spread that the house had been sold to a black family, the former owner's life was threatened, and Sweet knew he might face opposition to his presence. Determined not to be cowed by threats of violence, Sweet moved his possessions into his new home. He also brought some weapons and asked some friends to stay for a few days. The situation was so tense that the Detroit police office stationed a round-the-clock guard.

Soon, a large mob had gathered outside the Sweet home. Insults were yelled and rocks tossed at the house as Sweet and his friends waited inside. After an uneasy day and night, the mob finally rushed the house. Sweet and another man fired their weapons from the second floor windows, killing one man and wounding another. Only then did the police act, storming the house and arresting everyone inside for murder.

Defense attorney Clarence Darrow gained notoriety not only for his success with the Sweet case but also for the highly publicized 1925 Scopes-Monkey trial, which debated the issue of teaching evolution in schools. *(Library of Congress)*

The NAACP immediately hired Clarence Darrow, one of America's most famed defense attorneys, to handle the case. The trial was followed closely around the country, and when Darrow eventually succeeded in winning acquittal for the Sweets, it was headline news— but only in the black papers.

Wilkins covered the case thoroughly in the *Call*. But when Roy asked an editor at the *Kansas City Star* if he had heard anything about the verdict, the man replied he didn't even know anything about the story.

For Wilkins, the Sweet case was typical of the inattention given to black Americans and their problems. No matter how eloquently he wrote about injustice, the fact was he still had to sit in a segregated balcony in order to attend a friend's graduation from the Horner Institute, a conservatory in Kansas City. That friend, the first black person to earn a degree from Horner, was also relegated to the balcony—the only graduate not to cross the stage to receive his diploma. As Wilkins and his friends sat up in the balcony and listened to their friend's music being played below, Roy looked down and saw a dark-skinned student from the Philippines seated with the other white graduates. As he later wrote, it was there he realized, "The color line wasn't really based on color at all: it was simply meant to keep down Americans who were Negroes."

Wilkins's time in Kansas City tested his faith in many things. His inherent belief in the possibility of integration was battered and beaten by the clear-cut hatred of black Americans he faced every day. His faith in the power of the press was bruised by the stone wall keeping stories about African Americans from ever reaching white eyes. But the fall and winter of 1927 brought the most difficult tests of all.

In late 1927, Wilkins's sister, Armeda, was diagnosed with tuberculosis—the same disease that had killed their mother—and died. Two months later, Roy's Aunt Elizabeth suffered a heart attack. When word of her illness reached her husband, Sam, he had a stroke. They died within two days of each other.

Roy was devastated. His younger brother, Earl, had just graduated from the University of Minnesota, and Wilkins wasted little time bringing him to Kansas City.

By bringing what remained of the family together, the brothers grew closer than ever before. Earl came to work for the *Call*, helping to sell advertisements. The two brothers spent most of their time outside of work together, too, enjoying what social life there was to be had for young black men in the 1920s.

The theaters, nightclubs, and restaurants of Kansas City were all segregated or white-only. Wilkins drew upon his experience in college, when he had been denied admission to a fraternity because of his race, and joined a group of citizens determined to bring popular African-American entertainers to town. Paul Robeson, one of the most widely acclaimed concert singers of his time, was the first celebrity to accept their invitation. Robeson, the son of a former slave, had graduated from Columbia Law School but now made his living on Broadway. His visit to Kansas City was something of a coup, especially since he was willing to reduce his usual fee to sing.

The *Call* ran lots of advance publicity for the Robeson show, as did the white-owned *Kansas City Star.* The only difference was that the *Star* did not run any pictures of Robeson because it still had a strict policy against putting pictures of African Americans in its pages.

Determined not to segregate the theater, Wilkins's group sold tickets for the show on a first-come, first-served basis. Though some white people protested, demanding segregated seating, Wilkins and his cohorts would not give in. As Wilkins later wrote, there was

Actor and entertainer Paul Robeson. *(Library of Congress)*

"quite a hullabaloo about the seating arrangements, [but] being a Negro community promoting a Negro artist, we could not (just from a business standpoint, aside from the moral values involved)—we could not agree to any segregation." They held out for an integrated show, and despite some worrisome moments, they saw the curtain rise on a sold-out house—filled with black and white faces alike.

Though the show was a success, it left controversy in its wake. Robeson, famous for his appearances in such plays as *Othello*, had chosen to sing only "traditional"

African-American music, including spirituals, which are deeply connected to slavery. His choice revealed a divide in the black community between those who appreciated the music and those who considered the songs lowbrow and inappropriate for a professional venue.

The *Call* ran some of the most strident criticism of the show on its front page. L. J. Bacote, a black music teacher who had studied in New England and Kansas City conservatories, wrote that Robeson's choice to sing exclusively African-American music was an embarrassment. In a lengthy article, she complained, "Since [Robeson] was advertised as a high-salaried artist, I expected to hear some classics." She explained that the classics, for her, were arias, ballads, and other European musical forms, "whether in Italian, German, Spanish, French or Russian—something other than the native tongue."

The *Call* then printed a salvo of counterattacks on Bacote's criticism. One reader wrote that if Bacote's training had led her to such contempt for her race's music, "God grant that the Negro may be denied the privilege of an 'extensive musical training,' and just sing for me the soul-inspiring Negro spirituals as they were sung by our fathers." The conflict mirrored one of the central debates of the time for African Americans, one that had been ongoing since W. E. B. Du Bois squared off against Booker T. Washington. Black Americans were caught between two worlds, with some calling for assimilation into white culture, and others urging their peers to hold onto their African identity. Wilkins had a front-row seat for the battle, but neither he nor anyone else had a way to solve the problem.

Wilkins's time in Kansas City was about learning to understand questions more than it was finding answers. Still a young man, he enjoyed meeting people and being exposed to all the ideas and influences he could find. He spent much of his leisure time at house parties, the most popular form of entertainment for blacks in Kansas City since most public facilities were segregated. A handsome man, he attracted his fair share of attention from the opposite sex. For a time, he dated Marvel Jackson, who would later become famous in her own right as a journalist, writer, and civil rights activist.

However, Aminda "Minnie" Badeau was the young woman who eventually captured Wilkins's heart. She was a thin young woman with olive-colored skin and large beautiful eyes, and he vowed to get to know her the minute he saw her across the room at a benefit fashion show. Minnie had just arrived in Kansas City from St. Louis, having been hired for a job with the city's branch of the National Urban League.

Founded in 1910 as the Committee on Urban Conditions among Negroes, the League had evolved into an organization devoted to helping blacks who had come north during the migration of the early twentieth century. It encouraged economic self-reliance, focusing on helping blacks find jobs in the cities, but it also expanded its mission to include civil rights.

Minnie and Roy had similar backgrounds: she, too, was from a relatively well-off family and had chosen to devote her energies to the fight for equality and justice for all. She told him about growing up in a prominent neighborhood in St. Louis, where she had white friends and met some of the most famous African-American activists in the country, including Booker T. Washington. The young couple hit it off right away, enjoy-

Minnie Badeau in 1928, the year before she married Wilkins.

ing a happy courtship. Roy took Minnie to the Eblon Theatre, where they watched movies to the accompaniment of an organ played by Count Basie, who would go on to become a great performer on Broadway. Wilkins accompanied her to parties and carefully steered her away from other suitors.

Wilkins had one particularly difficult obstacle to overcome in his pursuit of Minnie: her mother. Minnie's mother disapproved of Roy on several counts. For one, she thought newspaper reporters disreputable. She also did not want her Catholic daughter to marry a Protestant. Luckily for Wilkins, his beloved was not afraid to deny her mother's wishes. After Roy proposed, on September 15, 1929, they married that same afternoon. They waited a few weeks to tell Minnie's mother, and she gradually came to accept her new son-in-law. The young couple was delightfully happy—despite the loss of his sister and foster parents, Wilkins was beginning to feel like part of a family again.

Five

Time for Change

In the spring of 1929, Roy Wilkins made his first visit to New York City. There he experienced the glories of the Harlem Renaissance—he saw plays (and was allowed to sit anywhere he wanted in the theater), attended dances, and enjoyed seeing comfortably integrated people everywhere he turned. He returned from his trip more open than ever to the possibility of leaving Kansas City.

That fall, the American stock market crashed in one of the worst catastrophes in the nation's economic history. As word of the crash spread, investors rushed to banks to try to withdraw their money. By 1933, 11,000 of the nation's 25,000 banks had closed for lack of funds. Millions of people lost everything. Spending dropped, causing factories and stores to close. More

The African-American painter Jacob Lawrence was famous for his depiction of the poverty that ravaged Harlem during the Great Depression. *(Photograph courtesy of Gwendolyn Knight Lawrence / Art Resource.)*

than a quarter of American workers lost their jobs. It would be years before the country recovered.

African Americans were among the hardest hit by the Depression. Many of them already lived in poverty or were just keeping their heads above water financially. By 1930, unemployment had reached 50 percent among black workers. Suddenly, groups like the NAACP had even more work to do and less funds with which to do it. As secretary of the Kansas City branch, Wilkins saw the challenges the Depression brought. His office was inundated by complaints and stories of African Americans who had lost their jobs. But he also saw the people who promised to try to help. One of those people was Walter White.

Wilkins first saw White speak at Linwood Christian Church in Kansas City. Linwood was headed by a white pastor whom Wilkins had long admired for his brave sermons against segregation and discrimination. The evening that White rose to speak, the Linwood church was packed with nearly a thousand people—almost all of them white. The man they came to see was the field secretary of the NAACP, a position that combined travel around the country with countless speeches and investigations. Walter White was aided in his task by his appearance—though he was born to black parents and attended segregated schools in the South, he had blue eyes, blond hair, and was easily able to pass as white. White people often mistook him for one of their own and were much more likely to confide in him than they would have been had they realized he was black: "Nothing contributes so much to the continued life of an investigator of lynchings and his tranquil possession of all his limbs as the obtuseness of the lynchers themselves," White wrote. "Like most boastful people who practice direct action when it involves no personal risk, they just can't help talk about their deeds to any person who manifests even the slightest interest in them."

Walter White, executive secretary of the NAACP. *(Library of Congress)*

White traveled extensively, collecting eyewitness accounts from both black and white Southerners, and turned
in his reports to the New York office. NAACP officials used
White's reports as dramatic and repugnant evidence against
lynching in their campaign against the practice.

White was often asked why he chose to live as a black man instead of taking advantage of being able to pass for white. His answer was always the same: he told listeners the story of an experience he had in 1906, when he was thirteen. That year, false rumors about violence committed by black men inflamed a riot in Atlanta. Mobs roamed black neighborhoods with guns and torches, burning down houses at random. The White family watched from their windows, the boys holding shotguns, as the crowd approached their house on Peachtree Street.

"In a very few minutes, the vanguard of the mob, some of them bearing torches, appeared," White wrote in his memoirs. "A voice which we recognized as that of the son of the grocer with whom we had traded for many years yelled 'That's where the nigger mail carrier lives! Let's burn it down! It's too nice for a nigger to live in!'" White recalled his father saying, "Son, don't shoot until the first man puts his foot on the lawn and then— don't you miss."

Luckily for the Whites, the mob retreated. But other families were not as fortunate. It struck Walter White deeply that every black person was in danger just because of the color of his skin, and he took every opportunity he could find to pass the lesson onto others.

White's gifts as a public speaker greatly moved the crowd at the Linwood church. Wilkins was especially taken by the passionate oration and made a special effort to talk to White during his stay in Kansas City. White wrote him a few days after returning to New York, saying he had enjoyed his visit and hoped "some good comes of it." Thus began a friendship and a working relationship that would shape Roy's life as an activist.

By the end of the decade, Roy Wilkins's life centered ever more closely around America's most important race issues. The *Call* gave him an outlet to publicize his rage at Jim Crow and discrimination, and his work with the NAACP gave him the satisfaction of doing something to help achieve equality. When, in the spring of 1930, Walter White put out a call for help with another civil rights campaign, Wilkins jumped at the chance to help.

In early 1930, President Herbert Hoover announced he was appointing Judge John J. Parker to the highest court in the land. Justices of the Supreme Court of the United States are appointed by the president and then must be confirmed by the Senate. Walter White sent a telegram to an associate in Greensboro, North Carolina, asking him to check Parker's background: "We want to be in a position to work against his confirmation in the Senate if there is any reason for such action," White wrote. There turned out to plenty of reasons.

Parker had run for governor of North Carolina in 1920 and had made his racist credentials plain to the voters. One plank in his campaign platform had been the disenfranchisement of African Americans, calling the black vote "a source of evil to both races." He was defeated in the election, but was given a lifetime appointment to the U.S. Court of Appeals for the Fourth Circuit in 1925. From there, Hoover tapped him for the

Supreme Court. On March 28, White declared the defeat of Parker's nomination as the NAACP's top priority.

The Supreme Court was very important to the civil rights movement because it played a crucial role in deciding matters related to racial justice. For example, the court had established the legal foundation of segregation in the 1896 case *Plessy v. Ferguson.* On June 7, 1892, an African-American shoemaker named Homer Plessy went to jail for attempting to board a whites-only railroad car. Plessy appealed his case all the way to the Supreme Court. In 1896, that court heard Plessy's case and upheld the original ruling, opening the door to legal segregation under the guise of the "separate but equal" principle. Thus, Homer Plessy could be barred from a whites-only car as long as there was another car available to him. In practice, the facilities set aside for African Americans under Jim Crow laws were inevitably inferior—if they even existed. More than three decades later, the NAACP dreamed of seeing *Plessy v. Ferguson* overturned.

When Walter White solicited help in defeating Parker from newspapers and activists across the country, Wilkins immediately joined the fight. The next edition of the *Call* carried the banner headline: "COUNTRYWIDE FIGHT ON PARKER." The paper ran Parker's picture alongside his 1920 election vow: "If I should be elected governor of North Carolina and find that my election was due to one Negro vote, I would immediately resign my office." An editorial in the *Call* characterized the fight against

Supreme Court judicial nominee John J. Parker.

Parker this way: "It all comes back to the basic principle so often illustrated in American history—only those great enough to be just to the Negro, the humblest of Americans, are big enough to lead the nation to its highest destiny."

Southern senators rallied around Parker. Northern senators, however, had more black voters in their states, in part because so many had fled the terrible conditions in the South. They could not afford to write off the concerns of African Americans. Fortunately for the NAACP, Parker had made other enemies as well. He had angered the labor unions, including the powerful American Federation of Labor, when he upheld the legality of "yellow dog" contracts, which forced job applicants to sign statements that they would not join unions if hired. Although the AFL was segregated and no friend to African Americans, it joined in opposition to the Parker nomination.

President Hoover and other Parker supporters expected the judge to cruise to confirmation. The NAACP's success in raising a controversy almost overnight caught them on their heels. The *News & Observer* of Raleigh, North Carolina, noted "a political cloud no larger than a man's hand a week ago has reached the proportions of a storm since the National Association for the Advancement of Colored People got actively into the fight."

In the end, the Senate voted down Parker's nomination, 41-39. Wilkins was delighted at the NAACP's victory and proud of the role the *Call* had played in it. More than ever, White's campaign had convinced him that the association was the strongest voice for racial justice in America.

NAACP offices across the country felt the financial squeeze caused by the Great Depression. The association's magazine, *The Crisis*, was particularly beset by funding problems. W. E. B. Du Bois had edited the magazine since its inception, and one thing he had prided himself on was not being financially dependent on the NAACP. He wanted the magazine to be self-sufficient so the NAACP would not have any leverage to dictate content. At its height, *The Crisis* had a circulation of 100,000. But by 1930, sales, subscriptions, and advertising had dropped so low that the magazine could barely pay its bills. On top of these problems, Du Bois's rocky relationship with the NAACP's leadership dissuaded the great writer from turning to the organization for help. Instead, he looked for support from outside.

Roy Wilkins's name was familiar to many people at the upper levels of the civil rights movement. His work for the *Call* and for the NAACP had not gone unnoticed, but it was still a tremendous honor for Du Bois to seek him out.

Marvel Jackson, whom Wilkins had dated when she lived in Kansas City, worked for a time as Du Bois's assistant. Because of her connection to Wilkins, Du Bois asked her to set up an introduction. As she later remembered, "Dr. Du Bois went out to make a speech in Jefferson City, and Roy went up to meet him. When he came back, he said, 'I like that young man of yours, and I'm going to see that he gets a job here.'"

True to his word, when Du Bois needed help with *The Crisis,* he thought of Wilkins first. He believed the younger man's newspaper experience would make him an invaluable ally for the magazine. Du Bois sold the staff at the NAACP on the idea and Arthur Spingarn, chairman of NAACP's legal committee, urged the magazine's finance committee to hire Roy, saying Wilkins should "share whole-heartedly the responsibility of running *The Crisis* with [Du Bois]."

Du Bois wrote Roy to offer him a job as a business manager. The letter from the nation's preeminent statesmen for African Americans' rights thrilled Roy. Despite having criticized Du Bois for his focus on Pan-Africanism, Wilkins still considered him a hero. If he took a job at *The Crisis,* Wilkins would be advancing from a regional newspaper to a magazine with national circulation. In his offer, Du Bois promised to let Roy do anything that was "reasonable and not antagonistic to our main object . . . to make the magazine popular."

If Roy Wilkins judged career opportunities solely on the basis of prestige, he probably would not have hesitated. But he always moved cautiously when he evaluated job moves, carefully considering the potential for future advancement and the offered salary. The striking difference in the lower-working-class environment he experienced in St. Louis as a young child and the one he had discovered in the more prosperous household in St. Paul had stamped him with a lifelong pragmatism. He loathed the idea of enduring the penny-pinching existence his Mississippi-born father had lived. The example of his uncle Sam was always foremost in his mind. Sam Williams had put his family first and always ensured they had food on the table and a sturdy roof over their heads. Though he and Minnie had no children of their own, Wilkins was determined to follow his uncle's example.

The more Wilkins thought about Du Bois's offer and the more he talked it over with Minnie, the more problems he found with it. He thought his talents better suited to writing and editing than business management. The salary was relatively meager. Du Bois offered him $2,500 a year, a sum that would have barely supported Roy and Minnie in the expensive world of New York City. Furthermore, he worried about working for the famously difficult Du Bois. Confused, Wilkins wrote to Walter White, seeking his advice. White was encouraging but not overly so. After much discussion with friends and family, Wilkins thought he had no choice but to turn the offer down. He wanted to be a newspaperman, not a business manager.

Wilkins continued to work with and for the NAACP, communicating often with White about upcoming battles in the ongoing fight for civil rights. Their next big challenge was to build on the momentum the NAACP had achieved in the successful campaign against Judge Parker's nomination to the Supreme Court.

In the fall of 1930, the NAACP targeted for defeat several pro-Parker senators up for reelection. Among them was Senator Henry J. Allen of Kansas. The Allen campaign would be a daunting task—he was an experienced and popular politician. He had served two terms as governor and been appointed to his Senate seat to fill a vacancy. The 1930 campaign would be his first attempt to be elected to the office.

Wilkins threw himself into the battle against Senator Allen. He and Minnie volunteered to drive Dean Pickens, the NAACP field secretary, all over the state of Kansas. Pickens was an electrifying speaker, adept at hurling caustic barbs at the candidate and convincing in his argument that the incumbent senator had shown his true colors by siding with a virulent racist. Running in a crowded field of candidates, Allen won the primary but went down to defeat in the general election. The loss was counted as another triumph for Wilkins and the NAACP in their campaign to bring the nation's attention to racism in its midst.

Though he was a fairly well-known and well-respected man in Kansas City, Wilkins knew racism as well as anyone with dark skin. That winter, he was detained and frisked by police as he and Minnie were trying to get into their car. The cops had mistaken Minnie for a white woman, and, as Roy later wrote, "couldn't understand what she was doing with a black fellow like me." The officers soon let him go and no one was hurt, but Wilkins filed a complaint with the police department. The com-

Minnie and Roy during the early years of their marriage.

missioner investigated and issued small fines to the patrolmen involved.

Episodes like this one, no matter how minor they seemed, continued to rankle Wilkins. He could not accept racism and discrimination as the only way for black Americans to live, but every experience he had seemed to reinforce that reality.

Soon after their unexpected encounter with the police, Minnie and Roy knowingly risked their lives to travel to Clinton, Missouri, to investigate a report that two black men had been unfairly charged with the murder of a white woman. The woman, an elderly shut-in, had been found dead at her home. The only evidence pointing to the arrested black men was a thirteen-year-old boy's report of seeing them in a wagon near the woman's home. Less than two days after their arrest, both men stood in a courtroom surrounded by a mob that cheered as their death sentences were read.

When Roy and Minnie arrived in Clinton, they found the black section of town almost completely blacked out. People were hiding in their houses with the lights off, hoping any passing vigilantes would think no one was home. Roy used his credentials with the *Call* to get an interview with the wife of one of the accused men. They carried on their entire conversation in the dark. Wilkins shook with rage as he heard the explanation of the way two black men had been railroaded for a crime they clearly did not commit.

On their return trip to Kansas City, Roy and Minnie

discussed their anger and frustration. Wilkins was beginning to wonder how effective another story or editorial would be in a place like Kansas City. He had job security and even some prestige in the African-American community, but he could not sit in the front row of a movie theater or eat in the all-white restaurants. He started to worry that by not doing more to protest racism and its effects, he was actually condoning it. He began to believe he had no choice but to do more.

In February of 1931, Wilkins opened a letter in the pile on his desk at the *Call.* It was from Walter White. James Weldon Johnson had resigned his post as secretary of the NAACP, leaving White in the role of acting secretary. The association needed a new assistant secretary, someone who could carry out assignments ordered by the secretary and take charge of the organization if the secretary's office was vacated.

White's recommendation for his successor would carry considerable weight, although the association's board of directors would have final approval. First, White wanted to know if Wilkins was interested in the job.

Wilkins was more than interested—he was ecstatic. He had declined Du Bois's offer because he worried that being the business manager of *The Crisis* would misdirect his skills. The assistant secretary's position at the NAACP would put him in the forefront of the civil rights struggle. It would also put him in a position to advance to leadership of the country's most effective civil rights organization.

He was careful, however, to preserve his bargaining position. He wrote back two short paragraphs, thanking White for his offer and explaining, "You may say to your committee that I am interested," then adding, "It seems wise to me to reserve any further discussion until a conference can be held."

In late March, Wilkins took the train to New York City to meet with the association's board of directors. The meeting went well until the topic turned to salary. Wilkins wanted $3,500 a year. The board would only offer $3,000. Disappointed, Wilkins asked for time to think it over and returned home. He still burned with the desire to get out of Kansas City and take up an activist career in New York. He discussed the matter with Minnie, and they carefully considered what their expenses would be.

Eventually, Roy and the association reached a compromise: $3,300 a year for the time being, with an opportunity for future raises. Roy then had to tell his friend and publisher, Chester Arthur Franklin, that he was leaving the newspaper business. Franklin tried hard to talk his editor out of the decision, but finally had to settle for a promise Wilkins would return if things did not work out in New York.

Minnie and Roy packed their bags and made their plans. She would quit her job at the Urban League and seek employment in New York. Wilkins said good-bye to his brother Earl, a difficult leave-taking; then he and Minnie traveled together to St. Louis. Minnie was to visit with her family for a little while before joining Roy in

New York. In August of 1931, Wilkins boarded a car of the Pennsylvania Railroad. As the miles of track lengthened between him and Kansas City, Roy Wilkins was headed toward the most important events of his life.

Six

A New Career

Roy Wilkins arrived in New York on August 14, 1931, with little more than his bags and the clothes on his back. His first order of business was to find a place to live.

He knew the YWCA in Harlem kept a registry of houses willing to take in boarders, and from that list he found a boarding house on West 136th Street. The rooms were clean, spacious, and well lit. He paid the first week's rent and unpacked. The next day, he officially reported to work at the NAACP headquarters at 69 Fifth Avenue.

The organization Wilkins had joined was the preeminent civil right group in the country. It was also the most militant, taking pride in its cutting-edge approach to attaining equality for all Americans. Individual chapters across the country sent information to headquarters, where Walter White's staff processed it and made plans

At its headquarters on 69 Fifth Avenue in New York City, the NAACP flew a flag to report lynchings until, in 1938, the threat of losing its lease forced the association to discontinue the practice. *(Library of Congress)*

for action. Despite the constant threat of violence, the NAACP sent agents into the field to investigate reports of civil rights abuses. Its supporters worked ceaselessly to bring the country's attention to the abuses perpetuated by a racist system. Though he had some regrets about leaving his beloved newspaper business, Roy Wilkins was proud to see his name attached to the organization.

Wilkins did realize the NAACP had flaws. One of the first things he discovered was how bureaucratic an organization it was. He was startled to find that, rather than having a frank discussion of the sort found in a newsroom, staffers spent hours behind closed doors polishing memos to announce their positions. Those memos led to more memos, which led to more memos. There was a good deal of bickering within the organization, and the sheer pettiness of the office politics could depress Roy.

As he tried to adjust to the way of life in his new office, Wilkins was relieved to have Minnie finally join him in New York City. They took a more spacious apartment in the same building and quickly set about getting to know their new home. Though the Harlem Renaissance had been severely damaged by the Great Depression, there were still plenty of exciting cultural events available for the young couple to enjoy. The Wilkinses were welcomed to the city by Roy's new boss, Walter White, who insisted they come to dinner parties and similar gatherings at his home.

Wilkins's duties at the NAACP varied. His position was a kind of catch-all job, doing every-

Wilkins in workman's disguise during an investigation of conditions on the Federal Flood Control Project in Memphis. *(Library of Congress)*

thing from raising funds to organizing new chapters to running the office when the secretary, White, was out of town. The two soon settled into a good working relationship. The same was not quite true of the other powerful force in the office, W. E. B. Du Bois.

Du Bois and White had long engaged in a power struggle over the leadership of the association. In March of 1931, the association removed the term "acting" from Walter White's title. Du Bois, at sixty-three the elder statesman of the association, complained that White's own personality and goals had too much influence over the direction of the NAACP. White believed that Du Bois was too divisive and radical a figure to be the NAACP's leader. White's training in business—his previous career was in the insurance industry—put him at odds with Du Bois's experience as an academic. Du Bois saw the association as an extension of an intellectual movement to be led by the Talented Tenth, the most elite and intellectual African Americans. White ran it more in the style of a modern CEO, micromanaging everything.

The conflict between them simmered for years, erupting periodically over seemingly minor disagreements. When Wilkins arrived at the association, he was unwittingly thrust into the battle for control. Du Bois had high hopes that Wilkins would take his side since the former newspaper editor would surely appreciate the importance of *The Crisis,* but Du Bois's clumsy plotting backfired on him. Still, Wilkins showed his own naïveté and needed the careful judgment of his wife to help him extricate himself from a politically dangerous situation.

Soon after Minnie joined her husband in New York, Du Bois invited them for brunch at his apartment. It became clear to both that the reasons for the invitation were not merely social. He wanted Roy to join him in the effort to unseat Walter White. But he made a critical blunder when he took a phone call on an unrelated matter and began speaking in French, presumably to keep his business private. Minnie spoke French, too, and was appalled by Du Bois's airs and by his poor manners.

A little while later, Du Bois circulated a memo that was highly critical of the way the NAACP operated. When the paper crossed Wilkins's desk, he added his name to the list of signatures. That night, he mentioned the incident to Minnie. She was quick to realize the memo was a veiled attack on Walter White and encouraged Roy to remove his name from it the next day.

Roy had sacrificed security in Kansas City for the NAACP job. He made some missteps in finding his feet, but one thing he knew was that he did not want to be caught in a battle between White and Du Bois. But just as Wilkins's reserved personality could make him seem aloof, his backpedaling over the memo made him seem as though he was playing both ends against the middle.

Du Bois's perception of Roy as a cagey careerist spread to some other members of the staff. Some of the employees who signed his memo later lost their jobs. Wilkins was not among them, possibly because he had taken his name off at the last minute. Du Bois complained that some board members were "trying to put White and Wilkins in control [of *The Crisis*] . . . and still carry my name on the flagpole." He declared he would not work with Roy unless he was clearly placed as Du Bois's subordinate. "You see," he told another association executive, "Wilkins is White's errand boy," and added, "[Wilkins] does not have my confidence."

The ultimate tragedy in this situation was that Roy admired both men and would continue to do so for the rest of his life. He had not come to New York to take part in interoffice wars. He wanted to play a national role in the struggle for racial justice. He would get his chance to achieve his goals, but he would have do so while navigating treacherous political territory.

Despite Du Bois's mistrust of him, Roy became a member of the group appointed by the NAACP to turn *The Crisis* around. Its circulation had sunk from a high of 100,000 to about 12,000. Wilkins drew upon his experience in the newspaper business to think of ways to draw in new readers. Though Du Bois preferred to see the pages filled with intellectually stimulating essays, Wilkins helped to convince him to expand the magazine's focus to sports and human interest stories as well. He knew that African Americans would flock to any publication that was willing to put their own experiences and stories on the front page.

One of the stories that Wilkins was most proud to bring to the pages of *The Crisis* was about the so-called Bonus Marchers. Veterans of the First World War, they

The Bonus Marchers rally on the steps of the Capitol building in Washington, D.C. *(Library of Congress)*

were due to be given bonuses for their service beginning in 1945. Suffering from the effects of the Great Depression, the men needed that money sooner. In the spring of 1932, they organized a massive march on Washington to appeal to the mercy of the government. Wilkins traveled to the capital to report on the events.

The marchers had set up a tent city at Anacostia Flats near the Washington Monument. When Wilkins arrived there, he was surprised to find a fully integrated little city, nearly 10,000 people strong. Many marchers had brought their families along; black and white men, women, and children were living, eating, playing, and protesting side by side.

"In a mess kitchen which served only Southerners I saw Negroes and whites mixed together in line and grouped together eating," he wrote in *The Crisis*. "I was told there had been a few personal fights and a few hard words passed, but the attitude of the die-hard, strictly Jim Crow whites had not been adopted officially. Such Southern whites as I met showed the greatest courtesy and mingled freely with the Negroes."

He discovered an even more astonishing fact as he interviewed the men about their trip to Washington. Many of them, both whites and blacks, had traveled through Southern states together. They had hiked together and been served meals in white restaurants. Whites sympathetic to their cause had suspended segregation for the veterans.

"The [marchers] proved that Negroes and whites can do all these things together, that even Negroes and white Southerners can do them together," Wilkins wrote. This was the kind of writing Wilkins had perfected in Kansas City, the firsthand story that let him put his on-the-spot impressions into vivid images for readers. Du Bois did not write those kinds of stories himself, but, to his credit, made space for Wilkins's accounts in *The Crisis*.

Unfortunately, the Bonus March came to a tragic end. Congress rejected a measure that would have allocated bonuses immediately. The marchers kept their vigil until Congress adjourned and all hope seemed to be lost. Still, thousands of veterans stayed on—many had nowhere else to go.

Wilkins finished his article and returned to New York City. Shortly thereafter, President Herbert Hoover ordered the U.S. Army to drive the veterans out of their encampment. In the process, several people (including two babies) were killed, and the tent city burned to the ground. The sight of impoverished vets being assaulted by their own brothers-in-arms did nothing to improve Hoover's popularity, already at a low ebb because of the Depression. In the pages of *The Crisis,* Du Bois urged his defeat in the 1932 election. Democrat Franklin Delano Roosevelt was swept into office on his promises to revive America's economy.

In the meantime, Wilkins and the NAACP continued to use legal and social pressure to try to achieve their goals. When Will Rogers, America's most famed humorist, repeatedly used the word "nigger" in his first show on the NBC radio network, Wilkins was among those who did not find it very funny. He organized a campaign of protest telegrams. He sent them not only to the network but also to the show's sponsor, Gulf Oil. NBC executives claimed they could not stop Rogers from exercising his First Amendment rights, but in succeeding shows Rogers could be heard using the word "darky" instead. This small victory was tempered by a defeat when, two weeks later, NBC radio aired a show about the NAACP's twenty-fifth anniversary but refused to allow any mention of segregation or lynchings. Wilkins was never able to escape society's power in writing its own version of history.

In the summer of 1932, Roy and Minnie moved to 409 Edgecomb, an apartment building that offered such luxuries as elevators, carpets, and fresh-cut flowers in

Roy and Minnie in their apartment at 409 Edgecomb in Harlem.

the lobby. Harlem was not the place it had been during the renaissance, but there was still plenty to do and see. Walter White and his wife lived in the same building, where there were often dinners and parties with artists and other social activists. Wilkins later wrote that living at Edgecomb transformed his and Minnie's life—it made them part of a community and gave them a place they finally felt comfortable calling home.

As Wilkins began to establish himself as a leader at the NAACP, one of his main challenges was negotiating the territory between White and Du Bois. Though he thought both men were invaluable to the movement and to the association, he would realize they were both human. A case involving nine men known collectively as the "Scottsboro Boys" would bring Wilkins and White into their first major conflict and remind Roy, once again, that even though the problems of racism were easy to identify, it was not always easy to agree on solutions.

The case of the "Scottsboro Boys" first hit the news as Wilkins was being offered the job at the NAACP, in March of 1931. The sheriff of Scottsboro, Alabama, acting on a tip, stopped a train and found a group of nine black men who had illegally stowed away. With the men were two white women, both dressed in caps and overalls. They were Nancy Bates and Victoria White, two prostitutes from nearby Huntsville. Fearing they would be arrested, they told the police that all nine men had raped them.

Medical evidence refuted the claim, but the authorities were quick to believe the accusations. All nine men were arrested and charged. Nancy Bates would later recant her story and became a speaker at rallies to free the "Scottsboro Boys," but by then it was too late. (They were called the "Scottsboro Boys" not only because of their youth—the youngest was only twelve—but also because of the then-common practice of referring to adult black men as "boys.")

The Scottsboro defendants were brought to trial quickly. Alabamans seized on the appearance of due process to point out that not all black suspects faced lynch mobs—some of them saw juries. The governor even sent in one hundred Alabama National Guardsmen to keep the situation under control. But the kind of justice the Scottsboro nine received was barely better than a lynching. The NAACP hired a lawyer named Stephen Roddy to defend them, but Roddy offered a poor defense. He did not even see his clients until the day of the trial, and then he showed up drunk. Fifteen days after being charged, all but one of the Scottsboro nine had been sentenced to death. After decades of lynchings and lightning-swift convictions of black defendants, this case appeared to be yet another courtroom atrocity in the South.

Beyond that, there were things about the Scottsboro trials that troubled Wilkins. The case seemed cut to order for the NAACP's campaign against Jim Crow "justice," yet Walter White had delayed hiring a lawyer. Though the situation seemed tailor-made for press conferences

The nine "Scottsboro Boys" and their attorney, surrounded by guards. *(Library of Congress)*

and protests, White did not go to Alabama until more than a month after the initial arrests. White did not keep very close tabs on Roddy, asking him only to send his case notes to the head office for their files.

White's behavior became even stranger when he commented publicly on the case. He made much of the fact that the defendants were illiterate and gullible, even saying that some of the blame for the incident should be placed on "the ignorance and stupidity of the boys' parents." Some of his critics charged that White, with his middle-class background and education, did not feel comfortable having to defend hoboes. It was an uncomfortable time for Wilkins, who shared a similarly privileged background but did not feel comfortable placing responsibility for this miscarriage of justice on its victims. Because the NAACP dragged its feet in providing full support for the Scottsboro nine, their defense was taken over by the American Communist Party.

Communist philosophy held that land and property should be owned in common by the workers, rather than a minority of wealthy people or large companies, and that prices for goods should be set by the state. In contrast, America's economy was based on capitalism, which respected private property as a basic right and allowed free markets to set prices. In the 1930s, the Communist philosophy seemed attractive to many Americans who thought the Depression had demonstrated the failure of capitalism. Novelists, artists, screenwriters, and college professors joined or sympathized with the Communists. Communism was also attractive to many African Americans who were wooed by the promise of equality for all. Savvy party organizers used high-profile social causes to strengthen their base of support.

Wilkins was among those Americans who wanted no part of communism. He believed in free enterprise and most other American institutions. Despite his struggle against American racism, he considered himself a patriot. Later in life, he admitted he still felt sentimental when he looked upon the Statue of Liberty. He felt African Americans could prosper if accorded the same legal protections as whites. The working-class neighborhood he had grown up in taught Wilkins that people could achieve their goals if they were willing to work for them. Wilkins saw communism as a perversion of that work ethic and was saddened to see people fall for what he believed were false promises.

Top attorneys from the International Labor Defense (ILD), the legal branch of the American Communist Party, showed up in Alabama as soon as the news about the Scottsboro verdicts spread. They framed the case on their own terms, making it less a matter of race than about America's harsh treatment of its working class. The ILD lawyers immediately began the appeal process of the judge's initial decision. They also organized the same parents White had maligned and sent them on speaking tours through American and European cities.

Wilkins followed the case closely in the papers and through word of mouth. He became increasingly concerned that the ILD lawyers were winning African Americans' hearts and minds with their very spirited and public defense. Wilkins had to worry about practical matters, too, including a possible decline in membership if the NAACP did not make a strong showing in highly visible cases like this one. White's apparent indifference toward the Scottsboro defendants put Wilkins in a hard spot with his boss. He could never forget his loyalty to the secretary for bringing him to New York, but the Scottsboro case was the kind of injustice that he had crusaded against every time it came down the news wires in Kansas City. Wilkins told White that the association's near silence over the matter had reduced him to rewriting the Communists' press releases as NAACP positions. The association could not just record the case for its files, Wilkins argued. It had to fight as hard for the Scottsboro defendants as it had against Judge Parker. In response, White accused Wilkins of betraying him.

Though Wilkins was hurt and angry about White's attack, he bottled his anger and decided that it was better to work with White than against him. He had seen firsthand how the divisions between White and Du Bois had hurt the NAACP, and he had vowed to put the success of the organization over his own personal feelings. Wilkins accepted White's position and joined him to work on a campaign to pressure President Roosevelt into backing legislation making lynching a federal crime. The Scottsboro Boys would be left to the Communists for the time being.

President Franklin Delano Roosevelt. *(National Portrait Gallery, Washington, D.C.)*

Many black Americans felt they had an advocate in the new president. Roy was not so sure. He did not think Roosevelt, a wealthy, former New York governor, had any great concern for African Americans. Like most liberal politicians, he wanted the black vote but had no great passion to deal with the injustices that plagued those voters. His greatest achievement for blacks was appointing First Lady Eleanor Roosevelt as an unofficial ambassador to the African-American community. The First Lady made speeches to the NAACP and even attended an exhibition of anti-lynching art in New York.

But other than dispatching Eleanor Roosevelt for symbolic gestures, the Roosevelt administration stubbornly refused to assist in the fight for African Americans' equality. White did succeed in getting a meeting with Roosevelt, but the president insisted that putting anti-lynching legislation before Congress would only motivate Southern legislators to block every other bill he tried to pass. Following Roosevelt's lead, Attorney General Homer Cummings, at a national crime conference that addressed violations as petty as vagrancy, refused to address the problem of lynching.

Cummings also turned a blind eye to a particularly horrific race murder in Florida in 1934. Claude Neal, a twenty-three-year-old African American, was accused of murdering his lover, Lola Cannidy, a twenty-year-old white woman. A mob stormed the jail where Neal was held and seized him. Newspapers carried announcements proclaiming that Neal would be put to death, and a radio station invited white listeners to attend the event. Somewhere between 3,000 and 7,000 people showed up. After being tortured for hours, Neal was stabbed through the heart and died. The mob dismembered him and displayed his body parts as trophies. Yet Attorney General Cummings rejected White's pleas to use the power of federal law to prosecute the murderers.

This was the kind of horror that had so enraged Wilkins during his days as an editor. He urged White to authorize a picket line at the Cummings crime conference. White was initially reluctant to go along. The NAACP traditionally investigated lynching and other atrocities, publicized them in *The Crisis,* lobbied for civil rights legislation, and took cases to court. White was uncomfortable with putting the NAACP's name on a public protest that might resemble, if only on the surface, the kind of mob activity that ignited violence and disorder.

Having laid out many a front page himself, Wilkins knew sensational acts attracted attention from editors. He argued that not only would the picket line garner attention from the white and black press, but would help rally association members. White finally agreed. The date of protest was set for December 11. The protest group applied to the city of Washington, D.C., for a parade permit but was turned down. They decided to march anyway. Attorney General Cummings's crime conference began at Constitution Hall. Seventy picketers were there to greet him, FBI director J. Edgar Hoover, and other top law enforcement officers. Wilkins was among them, wearing a sandwich sign that read AMERICA NEEDS FEDERAL ANTILYNCHING LAW.

The police arrived within minutes. They tried to get

the protesters to disperse. When they refused, they were arrested. Wilkins and three NAACP branch leaders were among those taken to jail, and their arrests made the front page of the *Washington News*. Feeling the heat, President Roosevelt denounced lynchings in his speech before the conference—much to the chagrin of Attorney General Cummings. It was one of the association's great successes of the 1930s.

The NAACP still faced criticism, however, for its neglect of the Scottsboro defendants. Calls and telegrams poured into the New York office from NAACP supporters, demanding to know why it refused to act. White finally realized the issue could strike a staggering blow to the association's reputation. But it was not until the winter of 1935 that he agreed to let Roy represent the NAACP on the newly formed Scottsboro Defense Committee. The committee was made up of a hodgepodge of groups interested in the case, including both the Communist International Labor Defense and the American Civil Liberties Union, a group founded in 1920 to defend cases involving violations of civil liberties.

In the end, the Scottsboro defendants fared only slightly better on appeal. The state reduced the death sentences to seventy-five years imprisonment. Alabama released four of the defendants in 1937, on the grounds that insufficient evidence had been used to convict them, but kept the other five behind bars on the same evidence. To Wilkins's lifelong disappointment, it was twenty years before the last of the Scottsboro nine went free.

Seven

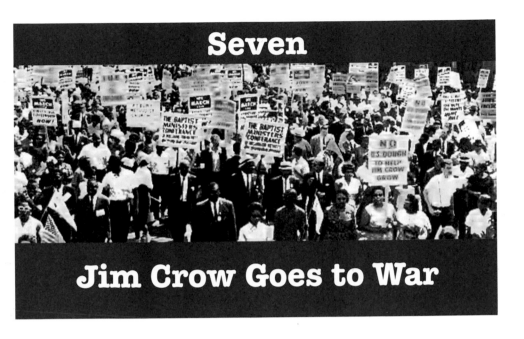

Jim Crow Goes to War

The tensions within the NAACP revealed by the Scottsboro Boys case would continue to exist for many years. Wilkins's job was to try to keep the organization active and effective despite personnel problems and the continual issue of funding. Dr. Louis Wright, a member of the NAACP's board of directors, summed up the trouble by saying, "the Association seems to be losing ground with the average man in the street because the work lacks inspiration."

Wright was not alone in his criticism. W. E. B. Du Bois was quick to raise his voice against Walter White's leadership and found Wilkins guilty by association. He tried to have Roy replaced as assistant secretary and raved that Wilkins "had neither the brains nor the guts to serve on any board." Still stung that Wilkins had first signed his memo against Walter White, then retracted his signature, he further denounced Roy as "a liar and a coward."

Du Bois, Wilkins, and White might have found a way to make amends and continue their work together had not Du Bois taken yet another step into radical politics. In early 1934, he published an editorial in *The Crisis* advocating segregation: "It is impossible . . . to wait for the millennium of free and normal intercourse before [African Americans] unite," Du Bois wrote. He went on, "It must be remembered that in the last quarter of a century, the advance of the colored people has been mainly in the lines where they themselves working by and for themselves, have accomplished the greatest advance." Walter White was livid. He demanded the right to publish a counterargument in *The Crisis,* saying that Du Bois's position did not reflect that of the NAACP. Du Bois refused.

Du Bois's statements were based on his belief that economic success was the key to political and social freedom for African Americans, and that the best way to achieve economic success was by not having to rely on cooperation with white-owned businesses. Few people were interested in the nuance of his argument, however. Most were focused on the contradiction between Du Bois's call to choose segregation versus the many years of legal, political, and social battles the NAACP and its members had fought to try to end segregation.

Wilkins was among those who suspected Du Bois's

statements were part of another power play aimed at toppling Walter White: "Dr. Du Bois's sudden interest in segregation was a declaration of independence, a test of Walter's power, and an assertion of Dr. Du Bois's claim to be intellectual leader of the race—a line in the sand."

Over the next few months, Wilkins and the rest of the NAACP could only watch anxiously as this battle was fought in *The Crisis* and at the association's headquarters. Matters finally came to a head when Du Bois offered his resignation, saying that he could not be part of an organization that would not tolerate criticism. Though Du Bois would be back, his departure was a severe blow to the organization's reputation.

Du Bois's exit from the NAACP dropped the job of editing *The Crisis* onto Wilkins's lap. Though he was frustrated to have more duties piled atop his already overflowing desk, Wilkins was excited about having the chance to lead one of the foremost black publications in the country. He was also nervous, knowing he had big shoes to fill and believing that any changes he made would be viewed with skepticism from loyal readers.

Though his appointment as editor of *The Crisis* was meant to be temporary, Wilkins would stay in that position for the next fifteen years—all the while continuing to fulfill his duties as assistant secretary. These were heady times—despite the setbacks and the trials Wilkins and his cohorts endured, there was a real sense that they were fighting for what was right and breaking new ground. Wilkins and his wife would not have children, instead giving all their time and energy to the causes they so fervently believed in. They were always glad to find new allies to join them.

One of those new faces was a bright young lawyer, Thurgood Marshall. Because the Roosevelt administration did little to back legislation proposed by the NAACP, the association was left to fight most of its battles in court. Marshall would become the organization's chief counsel and eventually have the distinction of arguing more than thirty cases before the Supreme Court. In 1964, he would become the first African American appointed to that highest court in the land. He was a slim, strong man with a thin mustache and a penchant for elegant suits. He used his agile legal mind to ensnare his courtroom opponents in traps made by their own words.

Thurgood Marshall during his early days of working with the NAACP. *(Library of Congress)*

Wilkins and Marshall first met in Baltimore when Wilkins made a speech to the local NAACP branch. The two stayed up half the night, drinking and talking, finding they shared common goals, values, and senses of humor. Their friendship would see the civil rights movement through some of its most important legal victories.

The middle 1930s saw several triumphs of black achievement in all walks of life. In sports, Jesse Owens won four gold medals at the 1936 Olympics. This was especially significant because Adolf Hitler, Germany's Nazi leader, had long touted the superiority of what he

Jesse Owens at the start of his record-breaking 200-meter race at the 1936 Olympics in Berlin. *(Library of Congress)*

called the "Aryan race." Owens's victories represented not just athletic records but human ones as well. The same year, the boxer Joe Louis famously knocked out the German boxer Max Schmeling, striking another blow against racism.

In 1939, Roy's brother, Earl, was diagnosed with tuberculosis, the same disease that had killed their mother and sister. Earl had stayed in Kansas City and continued to work for the *Call.* He married and had a son, Roger, on whom he doted. Earl initially beat out his doctor's projections, but he was always ill and spent much of his time in a sanitarium or at home in bed. Roy, inconsolable at the prospect of losing the last member of the family in which he'd grown up, traveled with Minnie to Missouri to see him.

Just as the Wilkins family was struggling to come to terms with Earl's illness, events in Europe were conspiring to bring on another war. Despite American efforts to remain neutral, this war would also reach across the ocean and drag American soldiers off to die in foreign lands.

In the fall of 1939, Hitler sent German troops into Poland. What began as a brazen landgrab quickly escalated into a war consuming most of Europe. The major powers were Britain, France, and eventually Russia, aligned against Germany, Italy, and Japan.

Wilkins remembered clearly the treatment black soldiers had encountered during World War I. They served in segregated units, were often relegated to menial assignments, and returned home to a new wave of race riots and lynchings. Though President Roosevelt promised to keep the U.S. neutral during this second war, most people believed it was only a matter of time before American troops went overseas. Wilkins wrote a letter to Secretary of the Army Harry Woodring demanding an end to segregation in military service, saying that he knew of "no single issue—except probably lynching—upon which there is a unanimity of opinion among all classes in all sections of the country."

Just as Congress steadfastly refused to pass a federal anti-lynching law, so arguments for integrating the army were ignored. Wilkins and other activists were bitterly disappointed, especially because the rhetoric used to justify support for Britain and France claimed that defeating Hitler was the only way to make the world safe for democracy.

As America anxiously watched events in Europe, Roy and Minnie experienced tragedy closer to home. Earl Wilkins was becoming sicker, and in January of 1941, he died. He was not yet forty years old. Roy's sorrow was mixed with bitterness when, after the funeral, he had to escort his brother's casket to a segregated cemetery. Even in death, black people were not good enough to be mixed with white people.

Earl left behind a widow, Helen, and a young son, Roger. A few months after Earl's death, Helen and Roger moved into an apartment building just down the street from Roy and Minnie in Harlem. Though Roy and Minnie never had children of their own, they doted on Roger when he came to visit. Roger would eventually become a civil rights activist in his own right, serving as Assistant Attorney General of the United States and winning a Pulitzer Prize for journalism.

In December of 1941, Roy Wilkins received an invitation to speak at a Washington conference on the service of African Americans in the military. He and Minnie took a train south to the capital. At a stop in Wilmington, Delaware, they heard devastating news: the Japanese had attacked the U.S. naval fleet at Pearl Harbor. The next day, President Roosevelt asked Congress for a declaration of war.

There is some irony in the fact that America's insistence on a segregated army slowed troop mobilization. There is more irony in the fact that America was fighting one of history's most murderous racists even while segregationist politicians fought to keep racist institutions intact in the United States. Some African Americans questioned whether they should take any part in a war to defeat a racist abroad while discrimination remained an everyday part of American life.

Another blow to both the war effort and to morale among black Americans was that most jobs in the booming defense industry were reserved for whites only. Asa Philip Randolph, the head of the first all-black labor union, the Brotherhood of Sleeping Car Porters, brought the issue to a head when he called for a march on Washington to protest discrimination at defense plants.

A. Philip Randolph, founder of the Brotherhood of Sleeping Car Porters. *(National Portrait Gallery, Washington, D.C.)*

A former magazine editor, Randolph had taken over as head of the black railroad porters' union in 1925, despite never having worked as a porter himself. He led a twelve-year fight against the Pullman Company for better pay and conditions. The company finally conceded defeat after a brutal and sometimes violent battle, and in 1937, it signed the first major labor settlement with African Americans in history.

Randolph was a tall, eloquent man with exquisite manners and a courtliness that belied a shrewd sense of politics. Eleanor Roosevelt was sent to size him up, and reported back to her husband that he would be dangerous to underestimate. Alarmed at the prospect of marchers, rioters, or worse in the nation's capital, the president asked Walter White to try to talk Randolph out of his plan.

Roosevelt did not know his adversary very well. Randolph was as stubborn as any civil rights leader alive. In his autobiography, Roy wrote, "Walter couldn't have talked Randolph out of that march even if he had wanted to—which he didn't—but he was too deft a politician to let the President and First Lady know that." White, too, reported back to Roosevelt that Randolph's threat was very real.

On June 13, 1941, Roosevelt met with a group that included Randolph and White in order to discuss the proposed march. Randolph made his goals clear from the beginning: "Mr. President, we want you to issue an executive order making it mandatory that Negroes be permitted to work in these [defense] plants."

Roosevelt replied that he could not possibly do that: "If I issue an executive order for you, then there'll be no end to other groups coming in here and asking me to issue executive orders for them, too."

"I'm sorry, Mr. President, the march cannot be called off," Randolph answered.

"How many people do you plan to bring?" Roosevelt asked.

"One hundred thousand, Mr. President."

Roosevelt was astonished. He asked White if the figure could possibly be accurate. White assured him it was. White had no idea whether Randolph could bring 100,000 marchers into the U.S. capital, but he was not about to admit that.

Roosevelt angrily warned Randolph that his march could get people killed. Washington was a segregated city and many of its police officers were Southerners. Randolph advised him that the best way to avoid violence would be for the president to address the crowd himself. Roosevelt refused. The meeting adjourned without resolution, but less than two weeks later it was clear Randolph had won.

On June 25, President Roosevelt issued Executive Order 8802, which stated: "[T]here shall be no discrimination in the employment of workers in defense industries or government because of race, creed, color or national origin." The order placed the burden of compliance on employers and unions, but Roosevelt also put in place the Fair Employment Practices Committee to enforce the new rules.

As he had promised the president, Randolph cancelled the march. Wilkins and White suspected that he had been bluffing about the 100,000 marchers. "To this day, I don't know if he would have been able to turn out enough marchers to make his point stick," Roy wrote

A poster promoting MOWM involvement.

years later. He was nonetheless delighted that Randolph had backed down the most powerful man in the country.

Wilkins had strongly supported Randolph's plan to desegregate the defense industry, but he was not quite as pleased with Randolph's follow-up to his success at the White House. Randolph established the March on Washington Movement (MOWM), a group that intended to keep the threat of a march active as permanent leverage against foot-dragging federal politicians.

Wilkins did not think every civil rights issue could be solved by a march. He also feared the MOWM group would split African Americans into two camps, and that march militants would undermine the legal challenges favored by the NAACP. Wilkins warned Walter White about discounting the significance of the MOWM and of falling into the "traditional NAACP attitude, namely, [believing] that these people are of no importance, and the movement is bound to fail, and that we cannot be damaged or our prestige or membership hurt."

The March on Washington Movement set up fund-raising venues around the country, such as this bookshop in Harlem, which also served as the committee's organizing headquarters. *(Library of Congress)*

White agreed. He, too, was concerned that the MOWM could end up draining resources from the association. He also voiced a fear that "some people [could believe] that the March-On-Washington Movement should replace the NAACP."

Wilkins had started out as a firebrand against racism in Kansas City, and he had joined the NAACP as an idealistic young activist. But in putting his concerns about the future of the NAACP above support for a movement ostensibly aligned with the same goals, he came across, at least to his rivals, as more focused on his personal ambition than the movement. Many people came to believe Roy Wilkins had transformed from race radical to cautious conservative. He didn't see himself that way, but the perception would follow him until the end of his career.

Eight

The Fight Becomes Clear

More than 500,000 black Americans went overseas during World War II, yet they served in the same segregated military their fathers and uncles had endured in the First World War. There were a few exceptions: the famed Tuskegee Airmen, an all-black squadron of pilots that flew important missions, and the 2,000 black soldiers who volunteered to fight when the army needed them most—during the Battle of the Bulge. But for the most part, there seemed to be few advances made in the fight for equality.

On the home front, dissatisfaction was growing. Years of experiencing racism and discrimination had not made them any easier to take.

In May 1943, African-American workers for Alabama Dry Dock and Shipbuilding Company in Mobile, Ala-

This picture of a group of Tuskegee airmen was taken by an anonymous photographer.

bama, demanded that more black workers be promoted to skilled jobs. The company responded by upgrading twelve workers to the rank of welder. The next day, thousands of whites attacked their black coworkers, clubbing them with pipes. A unit of troops from a nearby army base had to be summoned to quell the mob violence. The company suspended nearly 10,000 African-American workers in order to be able to resume production.

Violence was not confined to the South. In Detroit, Michigan, the city still simmered from a riot the previous year when whites had risen up in an attempt to keep blacks from occupying homes in the Sojourner Truth housing project. Though named in honor of a famous former slave, the project had been built in a white neighborhood, and the rioters wanted to keep it white. A local chapter of the Ku Klux Klan helped fan the sparks of hatred. The housing project was eventually integrated without injury, but tensions in the city were extremely high.

A year later, white workers in a Packard plant were incensed when three blacks were promoted. Their complaints touched off a storm of work stoppages and slowdowns, including a "wildcat" strike (not sanctioned by the union) during which 25,000 people walked off the job. White workers complained about sharing bathrooms with African Americans and about having to stand

A crowd watches as police officers arrest a protester during the Sojourner Truth project riots in Detroit. *(Library of Congress)*

next to them on the assembly lines. The United Auto Workers union, which supported interracial solidarity, called for the striking workers to return to their jobs. Packard executives secretly supported the strike—not for racial reasons, but because they hoped it would weaken the union.

By coincidence, the NAACP had just begun its annual convention the day of the walkout. White chided the company during his address to the convention, declaring, "Tokyo and Berlin tonight rejoice at the effective and unexpected aid given to them" by the Packard bosses. The union spared the city additional violence by siding with the black workers, ordering union members back to their jobs. Their hard work managed to keep tensions to a low simmer, instead of boiling over, but that spring nearly two days of rioting would result in thirty-four fatalities and nearly 2,000 arrests.

The Harlem riot came one month after events in Detroit. It started when a white police officer scuffled with a black woman, and a black soldier who happened to be there took the woman's side. The situation quickly escalated: the soldier grabbed the officer's billy club and hit him with it. The cop shot the soldier in the shoulder.

In the crowded neighborhood, rumors spread quickly, devolving into a story that a policeman had shot a black soldier dead. Mobs of African Americans smashed shop windows on 125th Street. New York City mayor Fiorello La Guardia called Walter White and asked to meet him at the 123rd Street police station. He wanted to confront the rioters head-on.

Roy thought that both men were out of their minds. He later wrote, "Walter was as white as La Guardia; how long either of them could last on the streets of Harlem was anyone's guess." But he rode in a cab with White the twenty blocks to the police station. White would later say that having Roy, a black man who looked black, in the car with him allowed them to pass uninjured through angry crowds.

Neither La Guardia nor White had much luck in calming the crowds. Wilkins joined Adam Clayton Powell, a New York City council member, and other city leaders who climbed into sound trucks, riding through the streets and talking to the crowds through megaphones. They assured the people that the rumors were false and no one had been killed. The message gradually restored order to the streets.

Wilkins saw the riots as a natural consequence of African American's rage at racial inequality. Condi-

New York mayor Fiorello La Guardia. *(Library of Congress)*

tions at home stood in stark contrast to the ideals U.S. leaders claimed they were fighting for. If Americans' sympathies were aroused by the fact that "Jews were beaten in Berlin and scourged in a loathsome ghetto in Warsaw, what about a tear for black ghettoes in America?" wrote Wilkins. White called the rioting "criminal and unforgivable," but agreed it could be traced to the deprivation and strain suffered by those living in poverty.

Germany surrendered in April of 1945, ending the European war. Japan conceded defeat in August, ending the war in the Pacific. Nearly half a million black troops returned from overseas to a segregated America. Though returning white soldiers were greeted with jobs and benefits, black soldiers saw less reward for the same service. The G.I. Bill, for example, offered assistance to veterans seeking higher education, but fewer black soldiers could use it because fewer had finished high school.

President Roosevelt died of a cerebral hemorrhage on April 12, 1945. When Vice President Harry Truman ascended to the nation's highest office, many black Americans were distrustful of their new president. He was from Missouri and had been a judge in Kansas City during the years Wilkins was denouncing the city as a bastion of segregation and Jim Crow. But Wilkins was familiar with Truman and thought his views on race were reasonable. As a senator, Truman had voted against poll taxes (used to take the vote away from blacks) and in

favor of anti-lynch-
ing legislation.
Wilkins wrote an
editorial in *The
Crisis* urging read-
ers to give the new
president a chance
on race issues.

A heightened
awareness of racial
inequality, along
with a resurgent
economy, helped to
swell the ranks and
coffers of the
NAACP. Wilkins
took advantage of
the membership
boom to bring the

Harry S. Truman took over the presidency after
Roosevelt's death.

organization up to date. The NAACP had 500,000 dues-
paying members, but only two field secretaries and one
director of branches. White was the only leader who
could be spared from the New York office for speaking
trips, but he also had to represent the NAACP with the
government in Washington. More staff members were
needed.

In early 1946, six black soldiers—still in uniform—
were murdered in Birmingham, Alabama. Police chief
Eugene "Bull" Connor was among the main suspects

(though he was never charged). In February, a black soldier named Isaac Woodard was honorably discharged from the army in Georgia. Wearing the same uniform he had risked his life in during the war, he headed home by bus to North Carolina. Along the way, he got in an argument with a white bus driver, who then called the police. Woodard was pulled off the bus and brutally beaten. His eyes were gouged, leaving him permanently blinded, and he was thrown in jail without medical attention. "We might have licked the master race in Europe, but our own master race pretenders down South had not begun to fight," Wilkins wrote.

Two weeks after Woodard was beaten, a petty argument in Columbia, Tennessee, escalated into a full-blown onslaught of officially sanctioned racial violence. James Stephenson, a navy veteran, accompanied his mother, Gladys, to a department store where she had left a radio to be repaired. She got into an argument with a clerk, who shouted at her, then slapped her. Stephenson got into a scuffle with the clerk and threw him through a plate glass window. The police promptly arrested James and Gladys Stephenson, released them, then arrested them again when the clerk's father swore out a complaint. The Stephensons posted bail and were released.

That night, a group of drunk white men with guns showed up in Mink Slide, the black section of town. They ran into a determined group of veterans who ordered them to halt, then shot at them when they refused. Word spread quickly and several hours later a unit of the National Guard rolled into Mink Slide shooting into homes and businesses. More than one hundred people were arrested.

The news reached the NAACP, and Wilkins pressed to send agents into the area immediately. Not only was this exactly the kind of abuse of power the NAACP was designed to combat, but Wilkins had reason to worry that if his organization stalled, Communists would claim the case for propaganda purposes—just as they had with the Scottsboro Boys.

Walter White had disagreed with Wilkins about the Scottsboro case, but this time there was no argument. White and Thurgood Marshall went to Tennessee the next week. When White met with the governor's secretary, the man sat with his feet on the table, contemptuously spouting racist venom. He did not apologize for the Columbia assaults but instead bragged about similar state-approved violence.

Marshall, along with two other NAACP lawyers, succeeded in getting all but two of the Mink Slide defendants acquitted. Those two convictions were reversed on appeal. Marshall suffered extreme harassment during his trips to Tennessee. Once, he was arrested on a trumped-up charge of drunk driving. He was lucky to be brought before a decent magistrate who smelled Marshall's breath, declared him stone sober, and released him.

Wilkins's work took a toll on his health, and in the spring of 1946 he went to the doctor complaining of a fever. An X-ray revealed a polyp on his intestine, a growth of tissue that needed to be removed. When the surgeons operated, they found the growth was malignant. Wilkins was told he would have to have a colostomy, an operation that reroutes the intestines through the abdominal wall. The body's waste is then excreted into a pouch, which the wearer can easily empty. Wilkins was horrified by the idea. He was forty-five years old and felt such an operation would disfigure him for the rest of his life. Minnie attempted to ease his fears, but Wilkins spent much of the summer of 1946 in a hospital bed, so depressed he did not care if he lived or died.

Wilkins was physically better by September, but still struggled with the psychological effects of his operation. Minnie attempted to lift his spirits with a trip to Phoenix. He had little enthusiasm for it, but she wouldn't take no for an answer. Reluctantly, he packed his bags and boarded the train.

Minnie fell ill on the trip and had to be treated by a doctor in Chicago. Their roles were suddenly reversed: now Roy had to care for Minnie instead of worrying about himself. Taking control of the situation revived Roy's self-reliance. Minnie soon recovered, and Roy never again felt limited by his condition. The trip proved to be exactly what he needed.

By the time he returned to the NAACP's office in New York, progress had been made with the Truman administration. The president issued an executive order setting up the U.S. Commission on Civil Rights (CCR). The

Wilkins holds up a noose he received as a threat while working at the NAACP.
(Library of Congress)

commission's tasks included an investigation into how the power of federal and state governments could strengthen the enforcement of constitutionally guaranteed rights, particularly for African Americans. The CCR was an important achievement, and Roy felt vindicated for the defense of the new president he had written in the pages of *The Crisis.*

In return for his support of the CCR, President Truman wanted the NAACP to back his global policies, particularly the Marshall Plan and the Truman Doctrine. The Marshall Plan, first proposed by Secretary of State George Catlett Marshall, was a proposal to rebuild war-torn Europe in a manner favorable to the development of democracy and free-market economies. The Truman Doctrine stated the duty of the United States to combat Communist regimes worldwide. Truman believed that the spread of Soviet Russia's influence could harm the national interests of the United States and democracies everywhere. The president sought to contain communism to the countries where it already existed.

Wilkins was glad to see the NAACP join the administration's hard-line stance against communism. White, too, was agreeable to Truman's global policies. So, in 1949, the NAACP publicly announced its support of the Marshall Plan.

Dissent came from an expected source: the unrepentant Communist W. E. B. Du Bois. Furious with White and Wilkins, he claimed the secretary had "loaded [the NAACP] on the Truman bandwagon" and linked it with "the reactionary, war-mongering colonial imperialism of the present administration." By this time, it seemed inevitable to Wilkins that there would be tension within the ranks of the NAACP, and he had begun to understand there was no way to make all the people happy all of the time.

Still, Du Bois's criticism was a bitter pill to swallow. An active writer and speaker well into his old age, Du Bois remained an important figure in the civil rights movement. Yet he and Walter White continued to bicker over philosophy, creating strife where harmony would have been more useful. Wilkins had long ago given up trying to please both men, recognizing that their outsize personalities meant it was impossible for them to work together.

Nine

The Top Job

In 1947, Thurgood Marshall stepped up his systematic attack on legal segregation. A skilled lawyer, he understood the importance of precedent-setting cases. He also knew that incremental steps, while frustratingly slow, were the best way to ensure eventual victory. That year, Marshall helped Ada Sipuel in her fight for admission to law school at the University of Oklahoma and Herman Marion Sweatt in a similar challenge to the University of Texas. Both plaintiffs were victorious, and Wilkins praised Marshall for his work, saying it "broke the ground for the attack on segregation at the secondary and primary school level."

That same year, both Walter White and Wilkins were beset by health problems. White suffered a heart attack, then left the hospital after only six days—despite his

The leadership of the NAACP in the late 1940s *(from left to right)*: Roy Wilkins, Walter White, and Thurgood Marshall. *(Library of Congress)*

doctor's orders to spend six months in a sanitarium. Wilkins wrote White to slow down and think of his health, then had occasion to take his own advice.

On a plane to Kansas City, Wilkins began to feel pains in his abdomen. He was treated by a local doctor and sent back to New York, where he was admitted to the hospital. The doctors delivered a grim diagnosis: terminal cancer.

They told Minnie he had only a few months to live.

Minnie simply refused to accept the diagnosis. She took charge of Roy's care, insisting that he take time away from work to relax. He submitted to her plans, finding pleasure in things he had not done in years, like attending football and basketball games. Soon enough, he made a complete recovery. The doctors called it a rare remission, but it's possible Minnie had been right in the first place.

As Wilkins slowly returned to work, a bumper crop of good news arrived in the offices of the NAACP. President Truman's Commission on Civil Rights had delivered a report that addressed the inequality that African Americans experienced head-on. In a document called "To Secure These Rights," it defined the American civil rights agenda for the next generation. The commission noted the many barriers against blacks and urged that everyone, regardless of race, color, or national origin, should have access to equal opportunity in education, housing, and jobs. Among the commission's proposals were anti-lynching and anti-poll tax laws, a permanent commission on fair employment, and a strong civil rights division of the Department of Justice.

In 1948, Truman also gave African Americans another victory by issuing Executive Order 9981, which stated, "there shall be equality of treatment and opportunity for all persons in the armed services without regard to race, color, religion, or national origin. This policy shall be put into effect as rapidly as possible." The

A large part of Wilkins's job at the NAACP was to stimulate the growth of the organization and promote NAACP membership. *(Library of Congress)*

military had finally been desegregated, and A. Philip Randolph's March on Washington Movement was responsible.

Truman had proposed instituting a peacetime draft that would require all young men to register for military service at the age of eighteen. Knowing that the armed services still discriminated against African Americans, Randolph brought the threat of a march to bear on the federal government. In a White House meeting, Randolph told Truman, "the mood among Negroes of this country is that they will never bear arms again until all forms of bias and discrimination are abolished." Randolph won.

Although he personally liked Truman, Wilkins believed he would not have acted without pressure from

Randolph: "There is no question in my mind that he helped push Truman toward doing the right thing, just as he had helped F.D.R. along on the eve of the war." Though he still worried about being in competition with Randolph's group, Wilkins also recognized that different means could sometimes be necessary to achieve the same ends.

Truman's support for the civil rights movement made him popular with black voters but triggered the fury of Southern Democrats. At the 1948 Democratic National Convention, a speech by Minneapolis mayor Hubert Humphrey urging civil rights legislation prompted a walkout by Southern delegates. They formed a splinter party known as the States' Rights Party, informally referred to as the Dixiecrats.

The Dixiecrats nominated Governor Strom Thurmond of South Carolina as their presidential candidate. He ran on a segregationist platform. Many political analysts thought Truman was doomed in the general election, worried that a split in the Democratic vote and the loss of the South would allow his opponent, Thomas Dewey of New York, to eke out a victory. The race turned out to be extremely close—the *Chicago Daily Tribune* famously ran the headline "Dewey Defeats Truman"—but in the end it was Truman who edged out his opponent. His win was due in no small part to overwhelming support from black voters.

But Truman's election did not bring much progress on civil rights. Southern members of the Senate used filibusters (not allowed in the House of Representatives) to stall civil rights legislation. The filibuster permits members to speak for as long as they like on any subject. In 1949, in response to the increase in civil rights legislation, the Senate's rules were revised to require more votes to end a debate. This hostility from the Senate reinforced the NAACP's plan to pursue the end of segregation in the courts.

In the spring of 1949, the NAACP was hit with yet another public relations blow. Walter White divorced his wife, Gladys, to marry a white woman, Poppy Cannon. At the same time, he requested a leave of absence from his position, leaving Wilkins to assume the reins and absorb what became a heated controversy.

Interracial marriage had long been a touchy subject in America. Many states had laws preventing it, and those laws would not be declared unconstitutional until 1967. (Alabama was the last state to officially remove anti-interracial marriage laws from its books, in 2000.) But much of the backlash against White came not from whites but from blacks.

The *Baltimore Afro-American* claimed White had "unwittingly placed in the hands of our most vocal opponents the very rebuttal they have attempted to use against our battle for freedom." The paper added that the NAACP and it members were "to blame for permitting a man who wanted to be white so bad to be their spokesman for so long. This error should not be repeated."

At a Los Angeles convention, Wilkins had to address

a room full of angry delegates who wanted to fire White for marrying a white woman. He persuaded them that it would be hypocritical for a civil rights organization to fire its director for participating in an interracial marriage. Wilkins's years of experience enduring the many feuds and crises at the NAACP had taught him that most controversies would eventually blow over or fade away.

While White was away, Wilkins made an effort to reach out to other civil rights organizations, hoping they could unite in a common cause. He organized the National Emergency Civil Rights Mobilization to pressure President Truman to revive the Fair Employment Practices Committee (FEPC), a wartime measure inaugurated by President Roosevelt. The FEPC banned racial discrimination in the defense industry, but it had been in limbo since the end of the war. Wilkins wanted to see the committee revived and made permanent.

He turned out a lobbying corps that included the Anti-Defamation League of B'nai B'rith and the American Jewish Congress, representatives of Jewish groups that had sided with the civil rights movement because of their own experience with anti-Semitism. The Congress of Industrial Organizations and American Federation of Labor sent delegates on behalf of labor unions. In his work with the Brotherhood of Sleeping Car Porters, A. Philip Randolph had persuaded union leaders that organized labor should take its place at the civil rights table. Four thousand delegates descended on Washington. Wilkins managed a White House meeting with Truman, who promised to help. In the end, however, the bill to revive the FEPC met the same fate in Congress as most civil rights bills: death by Southern filibuster.

The FEPC's defeat hurt Wilkins. His tenure as acting head of the NAACP was turning out to be a difficult time. Many people still spoke bitterly about White's divorce and remarriage, and some thought he should resign permanently.

The constant feuding within the NAACP leadership had clearly hurt the unity of the organization. The harsh words and rumors stung Roy: "One aspect of this whole situation that has been most distasteful to me and has caused me (for the first time) to become actually angry has been the campaign to discredit me personally, to belittle my hard work and my actual accomplishments, to say that I am not trustworthy, etc. . . . The purpose, clearly, seems to have been to force me out altogether."

White returned from his leave in 1951, and Wilkins gladly ceded control back to him. As with most of the association's infighting, the storm gradually blew over. But Wilkins's career would always be marred by opposing charges that he was not enough of his own man or that he was too much of his own man. Once again, Wilkins had to keep in mind there was no way to please everyone. All he could do was follow the example set by his uncle Sam: work hard and do what he believed was right without regard for what others said.

The 1950s saw a new development in the battle for civil rights for all Americans. Previously, the NAACP had issued legal challenges, held press conferences, made formal investigations, and given speeches. Protests had been few and far between, as the association preferred to stay within the bounds of the law. Large crowds were associated with mob violence, one of the reasons A. Philip Randolph's March on Washington Movement was so successful at backing down presidents.

As the civil rights movement gained momentum with legal victories and federal legislation, it spread out from a small group of elite fighters like White, Wilkins, Du Bois, and Randolph to become the work of the people. The methods of nonviolent resistance espoused by Mohandas Karamchand Gandhi, which had helped India win independence from colonizing Britain, gained

Mohandas Karamchand "Mahatma" Gandhi.

prominence as a way to create peaceful protest.

Martin Luther King Jr. was a powerful orator who tapped into his listeners' sense of justice. He and leaders like James Farmer of the Congress of Racial Equality (CORE) understood the importance of motivating people to demand change. In the coming years, they would step to the forefront of the movement with their emphasis on direct action and confrontation. The NAACP would suddenly seem like an old-fashioned, even stodgy, group. Wilkins would have to fight hard to keep the nation's oldest civil rights organization relevant in a rapidly changing world. The NAACP's most important victory came at the hands of Thurgood Marshall.

The case began in Topeka, Kansas, when Linda Brown, a young student, was told she could not attend her neighborhood, white-only school. The NAACP helped the Brown family file a civil suit against the city's board of education claiming that the "separate but equal" aspect of the 1896 *Plessy v. Ferguson* decision was unconstitutional. If schools were segregated, they argued, they would always be unequal.

The case was first filed in 1951 in the United States District Court for Kansas. It slowly worked its way up through the federal courts over the next three years toward a final decision in the U.S. Supreme Court. Along the way it was combined with other cases challenging school segregation.

On May 17, 1954, the Supreme Court agreed with the Brown family and the NAACP that segregation was

ORDER FOR APPEARANCE

Supreme Court of the United States

No. 436 , October Term, 19____

Office - Supreme Court, U. S.
RECEIVED
DEC 3 - 1951
CHARLES ELMORE CROPLEY
CLERK

BROWN, et al.

vs.

BOARD OF EDUCATION, et al.

The Clerk will enter my appearance as Counsel for the ____ Appellants

(Name) ____ Thurgood Marshall ____

Thurgood Marshall

(Address) 20 W. 40 St

New York (18) N.Y.

NOTE.—Must be signed by a member of the Bar of the Supreme Court United States. Individual and not firm names must be signed. Type or print name under signature.

The Supreme Court's order for Thurgood Marshall's appearance to represent his client in the *Brown v. Board of Education* case. *(National Archives)*

inherently unequal. In one decision, a century of school segregation was declared to be unconstitutional.

It was a shocking decision in many quarters. At the NAACP's New York headquarters the news was greeted with stunned silence. "The only emotion we felt at that moment was awe—every one of us felt it," Wilkins wrote.

As the initial euphoria of the decision wore off, the NAACP leadership immediately set about making plans to take advantage of the *Brown* decision. White and Wilkins spent much of the year laying out political strategy for the upcoming presidential elections of 1956, in which they planned to force politicians into taking a stand on civil rights.

Everything changed on March 21, 1955, when Walter White spent a normal day at the office, went home, and dropped dead of a heart attack. "Who but Walter would make a point of stopping by the office before going home to die?" Wilkins wrote, ruefully. The organization had lost a tireless and dedicated leader.

In April, the board of directors appointed Wilkins to fill White's position. Though the loss of his friend saddened him, he was elated at the chance to take the reins of the NAACP. As White's assistant, he was often stuck with desk chores and looking after small details. As secretary, he could set his own agenda, taking charge of the big picture.

He set his top priority as getting the other two branches of the government—the executive and the legislative—to follow the progressive course of action the Supreme Court had set. He planned to carry on White's goal to impact the 1956 elections.

Not long after White's death, events began to unfold that would push political lobbying into the back of most people's minds. In December 1955, a seamstress and NAACP worker, Rosa Parks, was arrested in Montgomery, Alabama, for refusing to take a seat in the back of a segregated city bus. Martin Luther King Jr. helped found the Montgomery Improvement Association (MIA), which began a nearly yearlong boycott of the city's buses.

At the time, King was best known as the twenty-six-year-old pastor of the Dexter Avenue Baptist Church.

Youthful, charismatic, and eloquent, he inspired crowds with speeches that borrowed the phrases and rhythm of the Bible. In a speech to his congregation, King praised the boycott: "And we are not wrong; we are not wrong in what we are doing. If we are wrong, the Supreme Court of this nation is wrong. If we are wrong, the Constitution of the United States is wrong. If we are wrong, God Almighty is wrong. If we are wrong, Jesus of Nazareth was merely a Utopian dreamer and never came down to earth. If we are wrong, justice is a lie. And we are determined here in Montgomery to work and fight until justice runs down like water and righteousness like a mighty stream." Almost overnight, he became the best-known black leader in America.

But white authorities were unmoved. In response, they issued the largest mass indictments in Alabama history, arresting more than one hundred leaders of the MIA on charges of violating the state's antiboycott law. In turn, the MIA filed suit against the city of Montgomery on grounds that segregation was unconstitutional. Thurgood Marshall quickly threw the weight of the NAACP's Legal Defense Fund behind the Montgomery boycott case.

King and another defendant were convicted for violation of the antiboycott law. Wilkins promised him the NAACP would pay all legal fees for both the boycott trials and the MIA's lawsuit against segregated busing. "We are quite conscious of our dependence on the NAACP," King wrote in his letter of thanks, noting that his church had just purchased a lifetime membership in the association.

King and other MIA leaders weathered threats of violence and intimidation as the boycott stretched on for months. Police harassed them with arrests for petty charges and nuisance tickets for minor traffic infractions. In January of 1956, bombs went off in the homes of King and fellow boycott organizer E. D. Nixon. But they persevered, and at the end of 1956, the U.S. Supreme Court ruled that segregation on buses was unconstitutional.

Wilkins *(left)* shakes hands with Martin Luther King Jr. and A. Philip Randolph. *(Library of Congress)*

The Alabama boycotts captured the attention and the imagination of America. Stories spread quickly of how people banded together, rising hours early to walk to work, pooling their money to buy one car to be used by twenty or more people, stopping to offer rides to strangers on the road. The NAACP was proud of the supporting role it had played, but Wilkins was furious when people suggested to him that perhaps he should slow down in his pursuit of civil rights. There were a number of people—many of them white—who saw the MIA's boycott as a dangerous development, perhaps even the making of a revolution. They had the temerity to suggest to civil rights leaders that they should, in the interests of peace and harmony, back off their pressure and give white Americans time to absorb the many and rapid changes of the past few years.

Wilkins could not agree more that times were changing, and he wanted white politicians to understand that African-American voters would no longer be satisfied with half-measures. He demanded that both President Dwight Eisenhower and his Democratic challenger, Adlai Stevenson, state their positions on civil rights before the 1956 presidential election.

The Republican Party had counted on black support after the Civil War. But in his first term, Eisenhower had done nothing for civil rights. Stevenson, on the other hand, had a reputation as a liberal on matters of race. In a meeting, he had impressed Wilkins with his grasp of racial issues. Wilkins hit a dead end, however, when he tried to convince Stevenson to make desegregation an issue in his campaign. The Democratic nominee was afraid an aggressive approach would endanger his support in the Southern states, and Eisenhower carried the majority of the African American vote in 1956.

Ten

Not Backing Down

In 1957, President Eisenhower decided to support the passage of a new Civil Rights Act. The primary goal of the bill was to protect the right to vote for African Americans. In its original form, the bill provided for the federal prosecution of anyone who interfered with any citizen's right to vote. The NAACP endorsed the bill, although Wilkins and others knew it would run into opposition from powerful Southern senators.

The bill easily passed the House of Representatives and then ran into a wall in the Senate. South Carolina senator Strom Thurmond, who had run for president as a segregationist in 1948, led a filibuster against it. The political environment in the country had changed since 1948, however. Most importantly, the *Brown* decision had placed the nation's highest court on the side of integration and full human rights for all citizens. This had encouraged many progressives and black leaders, as well as incensed segregationists.

It had also caught the attention of most ambitious politicians. In 1957, no politician was more ambitious than the majority leader of the Senate, Texan Lyndon Baines Johnson, who very much wanted to become president of the United States. Johnson knew that he had no chance of being elected president if he did not find a way to win votes in the North, and he would not be able to do this if he continued to align himself with Southern segregationists. He had begun to position himself as a bridge between the southern wing of his party and the northern liberal wing, led by the articulate Senator Hubert Humphrey of Minnesota.

Johnson also reached out to black leaders, including Roy Wilkins. He promised Wilkins to do everything possible to get the bill passed. The two met several times over the spring and summer of 1957 to strategize. Johnson also used the meetings to try to con-

Hubert Humphrey.

vince Wilkins to decide on an acceptable compromise. The NAACP would not get everything it wanted, even if it was right, Johnson said. The best long-term strategy was to get the best possible bill passed. It would be feasible later to try for a better bill, particularly if Johnson was elected president in 1960.

The biggest conflict was over voting rights enforcement. When it became apparent that the powerful Southern Democratic senators, such as Richard Russell of Georgia and John Stennis of Mississippi, would never let a bill pass that gave the U.S. Justice Department the right to enforce voting laws in individual states, Johnson begged Wilkins to accept a bill that at least officially recognized and ensured black voting rights. In other words, Johnson said a bill that formalized voting rights, even if it did not allow for their enforcement—no Southern state could be counted on to guarantee the right to vote—was better than no law at all. Eventually, and reluctantly, Wilkins agreed to the compromise and the weakened Civil Rights Act of 1957 was allowed to pass.

Many of the major papers heralded the bill's passage as a triumph for civil rights. The *New York Times* called it "incomparably the most significant domestic action of any Congress in this century." Most of the civil rights leadership, however, disagreed; several were deeply angry that Wilkins had agreed to go along with its passage.

Wilkins convened a meeting in Washington, D.C., to allow the leaders to voice their frustrations. They even considered asking President Eisenhower to veto the bill. Most of the black press was incensed at the bill and at the NAACP's support. "How silly can you get?" the *Chicago Defender* demanded. Wilkins was put in the uncomfortable position of having to defend a bill he knew was not good enough. He pointed out that it at least defended voting rights and established a Civil Rights Commission. "If you are digging a ditch with a teaspoon and a man comes along and offers you a spade, there is something wrong with your head if you don't take it because he didn't offer you a bulldozer," he said.

The same day the bill passed the Senate, King held a meeting that resulted in the creation of the Southern Christian Leadership Conference. The purpose of the SCLC, King said, was to enable black Southern leaders, many of them preachers, to organize to protect African American's rights in the South. Obviously, the NAACP had the same goals, and once again Wilkins was faced with another group that would sap funds and member-ship from the association. The formation of the SCLC and other civil rights groups was both a boon to the NAACP—they further legitimized the struggle—and a bane, making it clear the NAACP could not serve all black people and setting up conflicts within the struggle.

Civil rights critics and supporters alike had to agree that the late 1950s were a struggle. In the South, school districts were resisting the integration ordered by *Brown* as long as they could. On September 4, 1957, as nine African-American students prepared for their first day at Central High School in Little Rock, Arkansas, Governor Orval Faubus ordered the National Guard out to block their entrance.

As the troops surrounded the school, the scene outside Central High quickly turned into a media circus. Faubus took full advantage of the publicity he was getting—which he hoped would help his upcoming reelection campaign. A mob gathered, many of them shouting racial slurs and other invective. The nine students were sneaked into the school; then, out of fear for their safety, they were sneaked back out. Faubus's obstruction of integration was quickly turning into the most serious clash between states' rights and the federal government since the Civil War.

Wilkins sent President Eisenhower a telegram telling him that Faubus's actions undermined federal authority and urging him to intervene. He told an NAACP meeting in Charlotte, North Carolina, that those who preached states' rights over civil rights, a thin disguise for segregationists, were as guilty as the mobs: "The manicured hands of the solid citizens did not throw a stone or swing a fist . . . But their exhortations inspired less-restrained members of the communities to overt action," he said. "They cannot purge themselves by pointing the finger at another sinner, Orval Faubus."

Eisenhower had the National Guard troops removed, then responded to the crisis as though it were a military campaign, sending in the 101st Airborne Division. A thousand troops arrived in Little Rock in a day's time.

African-American students at Little Rock Central High in Arkansas are escorted into the school under federal protection in September 1957. *(Courtesy of Getty Images.)*

Many Southerners, whether for or against integration, strongly resented having federal troops sent into their states. Faubus preyed on their emotions, dramatically proclaiming, "Now begins the crucifixion!" as the soldiers arrived.

Wilkins responded to the governor's melodrama in more down-to-earth terms: "What baloney." Faubus was a strutting bigot, Wilkins thought, not Jesus Christ.

The situation dragged on for weeks, but eventually the so-called Little Rock Nine were able to resume the semblance of normal high school lives, and the first of them took his place among Central High's other graduates in May 1958.

The victory in Arkansas gave people real hope that, finally, advances were being made in the civil rights movement. But there was no time to rest. Wilkins, now nearing sixty, had been with the NAACP for almost thirty years. Yet rather than relaxing behind a large desk in a comfortable office, Wilkins was more like a rodeo cowboy—perilously atop a plunging, living animal, never knowing what to expect next.

When a jury in Union County, North Carolina, acquitted a white man for assaulting a black woman, the NAACP branch president, Robert Williams, told reporters it was time for African Americans to respond in kind and lynch the lynchers. Astounded, Wilkins called Williams to make sure the quotations were accurate. When Williams assured Wilkins they were, he was promptly suspended. The NAACP had to stand against lynching, no matter who did it.

Gandhi's message—that violence is best responded to with nonviolence—was spreading through the civil rights movement. As the 1960s dawned, a series of uncoordinated but similar protests moved across the country, all of them sharing a common theme: mass support and sheer determination.

On February 1, 1960, four students from North Carolina A&T State University took seats at the segregated lunch counter in a Woolworth's store in Greensboro. They were refused service but did not leave their seats. The next day, twenty-five more people arrived and took seats at the counter. They, too, were refused service but kept their seats. The day after that, more people arrived, and the sit-in spread to the counter at the nearby Kress department store.

The sit-in movement spread quickly throughout the South, and white people joined in. The premise was simple: take a seat, be polite, but do not leave. When the police were summoned, protesters were taught to either cooperate or, if they chose, to make their bodies limp, forcing the police to carry them away. They did not fight back and they did not protest their treatment. Arrests soon became a badge of honor.

Initially, the sit-ins were entirely spontaneous. As the movement grew, the NAACP offered help. Wilkins pressured the management of Woolworth's and Kress to end segregation at their lunch counters. He ordered NAACP branches to support the sit-in protesters, and led the NAACP staff in pickets of the New York branches of Kress and Woolworth's.

The sit-in movement helped push civil rights to the forefront of the 1960 presidential contest between Republican vice president Richard Nixon and Democratic senator John F. Kennedy. Kennedy endeared himself to black voters when he called King's wife, Coretta Scott King, to express his concern about King's arrest during a sit-in in Atlanta, Georgia. Kennedy had a generally good record on civil rights, having voted to ban poll taxes and for the Fair Employment Practices Committee.

But Wilkins still remembered Kennedy's vote to water down the 1957 Civil Rights Act. At a lunch he had with Wilkins during debate over the bill, Kennedy had promised to vote against the amendment calling for jury trials for civil rights violators, as opposed to court-ordered citations for contempt. But Kennedy broke his promise, voting for the amendment. Wilkins's relationship with Kennedy remained brittle for years.

Kennedy won the 1960 election, narrowly defeating Richard Nixon. He brought Senator Lyndon Johnson with him to the White House as his vice president. Having worked with Johnson before, Wilkins was optimistic he could help bring the president's attention to civil rights. Kennedy appointed a few African Americans to semi-important jobs. He also named Wilkins's old friend Thurgood Marshall to the U.S. Circuit Court of Appeals.

Wilkins was glad for the appointments, but he considered them a poor substitute for a civil rights bill. He wanted a bill that would give the Justice Department the right to enforce laws against racial discrimination and spell out federal punishment for states that tried to resist them.

Wilkins always preferred legislation and court challenges to protests, but he was still pleased by the progress the sit-in movement made. One outgrowth of that movement was the Freedom Rides, sponsored by James Farmer's CORE, which planned to actively desegregate public transportation in the South. The Supreme Court had recently ruled that interstate bus and railroad segregation was unconstitutional.

Taking their lives in their hands, black activists, along with white supporters, boarded buses into the South. The rides went peacefully at first, but the Freedom Riders soon encountered vicious beatings from white mobs. One of their buses was burned outside Anniston, Alabama. In Birmingham, several dozen whites attacked the riders two blocks from the sheriff's office. A mob of more than one thousand attacked them in Montgomery.

After the bus burning in Anniston, Wilkins and Clarence Mitchell of the NAACP's Washington office met with Attorney General Robert Kennedy. They demanded the government provide protection for the Freedom Riders. The new administration was focused on an upcoming summit meeting with Soviet premier Nikita Khrushchev—the Cold War was at its peak. The attorney general considered the violence down South a distraction, but Wilkins and Mitchell insisted the situation could turn into a disaster as awful as any mistake made with the Russians. Kennedy agreed to send the FBI to investigate and federal marshals to help ensure the riders' safety.

Kennedy's reluctance to help the civil rights movement came not from personal feelings but from political concerns. He was in favor of integration, equal rights, and other goals of the NAACP, and the violence in the South appalled him. But like other presidents before him, he worried about the possible repercussions of alienating Southern senators and congressional representatives.

A. Philip Randolph of the March on Washington Movement knew the only way to take the pressure from

Wilkins in his office at the NAACP in 1963. *(Library of Congress)*

Congress off the president was to put the pressure of the people on him. Early in 1963, he announced plans for a march on Washington to mark the one hundredth

anniversary of Abraham Lincoln's Emancipation Proclamation, the document that freed American slaves. The
event would come to be called the March on Washington
for Jobs and Freedom.

When Randolph asked Wilkins for the NAACP's
participation, Wilkins hesitated. Some of the organizers
wanted to use nonviolent civil disobedience tactics in
Washington. The NAACP had been law-abiding since it
was founded, and Wilkins felt reluctant to break with
that tradition. Though he appreciated the gains the sit-
in movement and other similar protests had made, he
would not put the NAACP's name on any illegal activity.
He and Whitney Young of the National Urban League
threatened to keep their organizations out of the march
unless Randolph gave his pledge that marchers would
obey the law. Randolph accepted their terms, promising
to rein in the militant members of his group.

Satisfied, Wilkins called for the NAACP to throw its
considerable power behind the march. At the fifty-fourth
NAACP convention, he told members the march would
be a "living petition for the redress of old grievances,
a march of decency and dignity." The delegates passed
a resolution of support.

As preparations for the march continued, a terrible
incident happened in Birmingham, Alabama. Martin
Luther King Jr. helped organize a peaceful protest of
that city's segregation laws. Police chief Eugene "Bull"
Connor, the same man rumored to have killed black
soldiers during the war years, gained instant notoriety

when he ordered the use of fire hoses and attack dogs.
Television cameras were there to capture the images of
people being shocked with cattle prods, washed down
the street with powerful streams of water, and perhaps
most visually disturbing, beset by police dogs. The
Birmingham episode had the unintended consequence
of bringing public sympathy to the side of the protestors.
Connor's virulent and unapologetic racism appalled
people and put a human face on the specter of hate.

Soon after Birmingham, Wilkins flew to Jackson,
Mississippi, to offer the NAACP's support to one of its
representatives, Medgar Evers. Evers had become a
national lightning rod for the civil rights movement
when, on behalf of the NAACP, he worked to have James
Meredith admitted as the first African-American student at the University of Mississippi law school. The
effort was successful, but ensuing riots left two dead,
and federal troops
were needed to re-
store order.

Civil rights activist Medgar Evers.

Undaunted, Evers
called for a citywide
boycott of segre-
gated businesses.
That led to violence
and rioting, and
someone threw a
Molotov cocktail
into Evers's front

yard. Wilkins came to town to show that the NAACP would back up its field officers in the face of violence. Wilkins addressed a mass meeting, then joined the demonstrations downtown. He and Evers were among those arrested for protesting. After they were bailed out, Wilkins returned to New York. Days later, word arrived at the NAACP that Evers had been shot dead in front of his home.

Wilkins returned to Jackson for Evers's funeral. He gave the eulogy, trying to find a way to see the good in such a terrible murder. "Contrary to the view of a Jackson city official, Medgar was more than just an opponent," Wilkins said. "In life, he was a constant threat to the system . . . In the manner of his death, he was the victor over it. The bullet that tore away his life four days ago tore away at the system and helped to signal its end."

Evers's death only strengthened Wilkins's belief that change was necessary. And he still believed that while arrests for a moral cause might get one's face in the newspaper or on television, they made little lasting impact. He still wanted a civil rights bill.

The recent wave of violence was making the government in Washington very nervous, particularly in light of Randolph's plan to bring a civil rights march to the capital. The president called the march leaders to a Saturday morning meeting at the White House to warn them a march would threaten a civil rights bill he had before Congress without accomplishing anything positive. But Randolph calmly and firmly insisted that the march would proceed as planned, and the other leaders closed ranks behind him.

On August 28, 1963, a quarter of a million people arrived in Washington. Almost a fourth of them were white. There were no arrests and the event went so smoothly, with such dignity, that it forever changed the public perception of the civil rights movement. Martin Luther King Jr. gave his "I Have a Dream" speech, departing from his prepared text to deliver a prophecy of a bright future in which all people would be equal under the law. King's speech was so moving that people in the crowd wept. Some white people who saw it on their television screens credited it for changing their minds about civil rights.

Organizers of the march join the energized crowd as they process to the Lincoln Memorial. Wilkins is to the left in this photograph, next to Randolph, center. *(National Archives)*

Wilkins on the August 30, 1963, cover of *Time*, just after the March on Washington.

Wilkins, too, could not help but be moved by King's words and the grandeur of the march. But after three decades of serving the NAACP, spending much of his time buttonholing stubborn legislators and putting in long hours on the phone, he knew that not all civil rights work was glorious. He intended to use his time at the podium to remind the marchers to keep up the fight.

Before he could deliver his message to the crowd, however, he had to announce sad news: W. E. B. Du Bois had died in Ghana, Africa. Though Du Bois had resisted joining the mainstream civil rights movement, this was no time to stress differences. Wilkins urged the people in the crowd to remember "at the dawn of the twentieth century, his was the voice that was calling you to gather here today in this cause."

Then Wilkins went on to ask the people gathered to remember the hard job ahead. "Just by your presence here today we have spoken loudly and eloquently to our legislature," he said. "When we return home, keep up the speaking by letters and telegrams and telephoning and, whenever possible, by personal visit. Remember that this has been a long fight."

When the march was over, President Kennedy greeted Randolph, Wilkins, King, and others at the White House and congratulated them on their success. It was a land-mark day for civil rights.

Wilkins was working in his New York office on No-vember 23, 1963, when he heard a radio report that President Kennedy had been shot in Dallas. After a flurry of confused reports, official confirmation came that the president was dead. Wilkins walked out onto Fifth Avenue to see people crying in the streets.

Vice President Lyndon Baines Johnson was sworn into the nation's highest office aboard Air Force One. Johnson had earned Wilkins's trust by leading the Sen-ate to pass its first civil rights bill, flawed though it was. In 1960, he had said, "Of all the men in American political life, I would trust to do the most about civil rights . . . it would be Lyndon Johnson." Senator Johnson had been a strong ally. Now that he was President Johnson, Wilkins could only hope he would not back down.

Eleven

Promises Kept

In his first major speech after Kennedy's death, President Johnson told the country, "[no] eulogy could more eloquently honor President Kennedy's memory than the earliest possible passage of the civil rights bill for which he fought so long. We have talked long enough in this country about equal rights. It is time to write the next chapter and write it in the books of law."

Johnson had long been an admirer of former president Franklin Roosevelt, who, while in office during the Great Depression, had passed a number of bills to help improve the lives of the poor and underprivileged. Johnson saw civil rights as an issue upon which he could put his own stamp and so mark his place in history. Still, Wilkins was surprised when the new president invited him to the White House soon after being sworn in.

President Johnson was famed for his ability to get powerful people to work together. He told Wilkins that he intended to put his vice president, Hubert Humphrey, in charge of pushing a strong civil rights bill in the Senate. "I want that bill *passed*," he told Roy.

The president proposed a bill that reached far beyond the half-measures of the 1957 civil rights legislation. It banned segregation of public facilities and accommodations, gave the Justice Department jurisdiction over school discrimination suits, and barred job discrimination. If states tried to resist, they would lose federal funds.

The bill easily passed the House, and the president prepared for the Senate battle. Johnson knew he would have to beat the old tactic of filibustering civil rights bills, still a favorite of Southern senators. He persuaded

Wilkins working with Lyndon Johnson at the White House. *(The White House)*

Senator Everett Dirksen of Illinois, the Republican Minority Leader in the Senate, to join in the fight. At first, Dirksen wanted to load the bill down with the same kind of amendments that had gutted the 1957 bill, but Johnson talked him into dropping them.

Johnson warned Southern senators in advance that he was prepared to outlast any attempt to sideline the bill. "They can filibuster until hell freezes over," he said. "I'm not going to put anything on that floor until this gets done."

He also warned Wilkins that the fight would be tough. "They say I'm an arm twister," he told Roy in another White House meeting, "but I can't make a Southerner change his spots any more than I can make a leopard change 'em . . . I'm no magician. I'm going to be with ya, and I'm going to help anyway I can." But he wanted others to do their part, and he expected Wilkins to both obtain the NAACP's backing and see that black voters remembered him in the election.

After seventy-five days of debate, the Senate finally voted 71-29 in favor of the civil rights bill. President Johnson signed the bill before a national television audience on July 2, 1964.

President Johnson had come through for black Americans, and now he expected the support of black leaders. As far as Wilkins was concerned, Johnson had earned it. The president, after all, had delivered the civil rights bill the NAACP had wanted since the mid-1950s. Johnson asked for his help in winning the 1964 election, and

Wilkins agreed. He and the president held strategy talks in which Johnson stressed that any sign of racial turmoil would hurt his chances in November.

Wilkins decided he would stick his neck out as far as the president had. He sent out a telegram calling for a meeting of African-American leaders, warning of "violent and futile disorder . . . if we do not play our hand coolly and intelligently." When the group gathered in New York, Wilkins surprised them with a call for a nationwide moratorium on marches and protests until the election was over. Whitney Young of the Urban League supported the motion.

The proposal touched off an angry outburst in the room. The NAACP had once ruled the roost of civil rights organizations, but by 1964, a host of new ones had been born, almost all represented at this meeting. King was there, representing the Southern Christian Leadership Conference; John Lewis headed the Student Nonviolent Coordinating Committee, a radical group that outflanked almost all others on the left; and James Farmer was still at the helm of the Congress of Racial Equality, an organization very much at the forefront of public demonstrations.

Lewis and Farmer angrily protested that such an agreement would choke off their ability to function. They also argued that if they accepted a moratorium, enemies of civil rights would classify even nonviolent protest under the heading of "Negro trouble." Even King fought with Wilkins on use of the word "moratorium," preferring the term "broad curtailment."

In the end, Wilkins prevailed but paid a price among the emerging black radicals. One of the harshest rebukes came from the leader of the Black Muslims, a group that urged racial separatism. Malcolm X, who had not been present at the meeting, declared that the leaders of the group "have sold themselves out and become campaign managers to the Negro community for Lyndon Johnson."

The Republican Party nominated Senator Barry Goldwater of Arizona to oppose Johnson. Goldwater represented the far right of the party. When Wilkins called the New York meeting, a Goldwater nomination had seemed the worst-case scenario for the civil rights movement. Goldwater's views on race were a throwback to the days when states' rights enforced segregation in every facet of life. In voting against the Civil Rights Bill of 1964, Goldwater had said the bill was "a usurpation of such power . . . which 50 sovereign states have reserved for themselves." Many people assumed Goldwater was too extreme to be electable.

To Wilkins's great relief, Johnson won a landslide victory that November. Johnson continued his push for African Americans' equality, seeking to make civil rights the cornerstone of his legacy. Wilkins's relationship with the president, popularly known as LBJ, evolved from that of advisor to close personal friend.

"I came away from the conversations I had with LBJ feeling he was not only with us but often ahead of us," Wilkins wrote. Roy's bond with the Johnson administra-

Roger Wilkins, Roy Wilkins's nephew, not only became an assistant attorney general but also went on to win a Pulitzer Prize for journalism and to edit *The Crisis*. He was photographed here in 2003 in his office at George Mason University, where he is the Clarence J. Robinson Professor of History and American Culture.

tion became a family connection when his nephew, Roger, became assistant attorney general at the age of thirty-three.

Johnson was by far the greatest president civil rights leaders had ever seen, but his presence in the White House did not mean the fight for integration and equality was over. The new civil rights bill brought a backlash, especially in the South. Alabama elected George Wallace governor after he promised to keep Alabama segregated. In response to Wallace's election, Martin Luther King Jr. organized a protest march across the middle of the state, from Selma to Montgomery.

Selma, Alabama, was a typical Southern town of the Jim Crow era. Less than two percent of eligible African

Americans were registered to vote, even though they made up almost half the population. The marchers made it only six blocks before they ran into police who attacked with clubs and gas. Hundreds were arrested, and the clash became known as Bloody Sunday. Less than a month later, the marchers regrouped and, in five days, more than 25,000 of them walked from Selma to the state capital.

Just months after the Selma march, President Johnson signed the Voting Rights Act of 1965 into law on August 6, 1965. It suspended literacy tests, which had been used to disenfranchise poorly educated African Americans. It called for federal examiners to monitor polling places to see that everyone was ensured the right to vote. It directed the attorney general to challenge poll taxes, another tool segregationists had used against black voters. The act was another tremendous achievement, and Wilkins's dreams of legislative redress were finally coming true.

Wilkins and the NAACP had long relied on lobbying politicians and challenging laws in their fight for equality. In the 1960s, a new generation of African-American activists emerged, and not all of those people agreed with the NAACP's approach. Some of them thought it was too assimilationist, too accomodationist, while others were caught up in the rebellious spirit of the times and saw the government as the enemy. Wilkins would be reminded of the terrible struggles between W. E. B. Du Bois and Booker T. Washington, and then between Du

Bois and Walter White, as he watched a new crop of leaders argue over the best goals and the best ways to achieve them.

Wilkins defended and admired Martin Luther King Jr. publicly, but he was often disappointed by the charismatic leader's speechifying. Wilkins believed that after he became famous, King became more interested in drawing attention, leaving the hard and inglorious details of the civil rights struggle to the NAACP and other groups. Once, in a low moment, Wilkins snapped at King, pressing him to name anything he had desegregated. After some verbal sparring, King finally said, "Well, I guess about the only thing I've desegregated is a few human hearts."

Wilkins would later regret this exchange. He knew King had an important role in desegregation, going all the way back to his leadership of the Montgomery bus boycott. In cooler-headed moments, the two men enjoyed a cordial relationship. But the tension between the movements in the streets and the movements using the courts would always exist.

Stokely Carmichael, director of the Student Nonviolent Coordinating Committee (SNCC, pronounced "snick"), and Wilkins also had a tense relationship. Carmichael was a militant radical who coined the phrase "Black Power." The Black Power movement urged African Americans to meet violence with violence. Carmichael preached black separatism instead of integration.

Stokely Carmichael, photographed here at age twenty-five, was the head of the Student Nonviolent Coordinating Committee. He introduced the phrase "Black Power" to the civil rights movement. *(AP Photo)*

Frustrated by Wilkins's close relationships with Washington politicians, Carmichael publicly called him an Uncle Tom, a derogatory term for a subservient black man who tried to please white people. Carmichael complained that "there was no give-and-take with Bro Wilkins. He clearly had no respect for the experience or contributions of any of us, not just the SNCC. In his mind, whatever the movement had accomplished—the legislation—was entirely because of the insider contacts and skillful influence of the NAACP. It never occurred to him that they had never been able to get any legislation—not as much as an antilynching law—until masses of people had taken to the streets in nonviolent direct action."

He went on to take a swipe at Wilkins's close alliances with President Johnson and other powerful politicians:

"I couldn't help wondering if he was equally imperious in the gatherings of the powerful and the wealthy he was so pleased to be invited to. Somehow I didn't think so."

Wilkins chafed at the criticism of his life's work, but he chalked it up to the generation gap. He recalled that he had been just as much a firebrand as Carmichael and other radicals in his youth, just as stinging in his criticism of W. E. B. Du Bois as a young newspaperman in Kansas City. "Times change; the souls of young men and old men don't seem to," he wrote.

The changing times also perplexed President Johnson. He expected African Americans to be grateful for what he had accomplished on their behalf. But young black Americans had little love for LBJ. As the president sent more troops to fight in the increasingly unpopular Vietnam War, his critics pointed out that blacks made up a disproportionately high number of the casualties.

Just days after Johnson signed the Voting Rights Act, the Watts ghetto in Los Angeles exploded in one of the decade's bloodiest riots. A routine traffic stop turned ugly—as police questioned two men in a car, a crowd began to gather at the scene. One of the men's mothers arrived, a scuffle broke out, and police arrested all three people. Residents of Watts had long suspected police targeted them for harassment and arrest because of racism. Joblessness and high crime in the Watts area had increased anger to the boiling point. Shortly after the police left, the crowd began to riot. Six days of looting and violence followed, leaving thirty-four people dead and causing $100 million damage.

Johnson appointed Wilkins to the eleven-member National Advisory Commission on Civil Disorders to help find answers to the unrest in the country. There was little that commission could do to stop the violence.

On April 4, 1968, a gunman shot Martin Luther King Jr. dead as he stood on the balcony of a Memphis motel. More than one hundred American cities broke out in riots. King's murder recruited even more black activists toward the extremes of militancy and Black Power. The assassination handed the militants a potent argument: King had preached nonviolence his entire career, only to be shot dead for it.

In the fall of 1969, Wilkins began to suffer pain in his abdomen. He checked into New York University Hospital, where doctors performed surgery to remove cancerous lesions from his intestines. Minnie suggested he consider retirement, but Wilkins was not yet seventy and believed he still had more work to do.

In 1971, Minnie retired from her job as a social worker. With more time together, the Wilkinses traveled, taking trips to Israel, Africa, Italy, and Germany. Minnie began to urge Roy to retire, to leave the NAACP's battles to younger activists. He had led the organization for forty years—wasn't it time for him to cede the reins to the next generation? But Wilkins was not quite ready to give up the work he had devoted his life to. He stayed on at the NAACP until July of 1977.

Roy Wilkins in the late 1970s.

The pace of the fight slowed for Wilkins, and he spent much of his time during his last years as secretary handling administrative work and making speeches. One issue he felt strongly about was the Supreme Court's 1969 ruling that school districts could use busing to fulfill the court's mandate about integration. His belief that integration was not only possible but also necessary gave Wilkins the strength to continue the fight. Though the glory days of the civil rights movement had passed, there was still the need for the tireless activism and attention to detail that Wilkins personified.

A constant traveler during his NAACP career, Wilkins became a homebody during his retirement. He wrote a syndicated column and took great pleasure in his readers' letters. He praised Jimmy Carter during the 1976 presidential campaign, and Carter repaid him with a handwritten thank-you note and an invitation to the White House to honor him for his work with the NAACP. Wilkins accepted the invitation but surprised the president by cutting their visit short. He wrote that he had suddenly felt very weary, realizing that the "civil rights movement was in the hands of others."

Shortly after completing his memoirs, Roy Wilkins died on September 8, 1981. In a career spanning six decades, he had led the fight to break down the walls of segregation, racial discrimination, and Jim Crow. The 1960s radicals who criticized him for working within the system never really understood him. Wilkins did not want to tear down America, only to reform it, for he was a true believer in the promises of its Constitution. "A racial minority cannot live except in democracy," he said. "In saving it, we save ourselves."

Timeline

1901   Roy Wilkins is born in St. Louis on August 30.

1909   The National Association for the Advancement of Colored People is founded.

1923   The NAACP holds Midwestern Race Relations Conference in Kansas City. Wilkins's coverage of the event earns him a job as news editor of the *Kansas City Call*.

1929   Wilkins marries Minnie Badeau of St. Louis.

1931   Wilkins becomes assistant secretary of the NAACP.

1934   W. E. B. Du Bois resigns from the NAACP. Wilkins replaces him as editor of *The Crisis*.

1954   U.S. Supreme Court strikes down "separate but equal" doctrine for schools in *Brown v. Board of Education*.

1955   Walter White dies. Wilkins replaces him as executive secretary of the NAACP.

1957   Lyndon Johnson leads successful fight to pass Civil Rights Bill of 1957.

1963   Wilkins joins A. Philip Randolph, president of the Brotherhood of Sleeping Car Porters, and other black leaders in the March on Washington.

1965   Wilkins joins King in the Selma to Montgomery March.

1971   Supreme Court rules that busing is a tool that can be used to achieve racial balance in schools. Wilkins leads association's campaign to urge acceptance and the decision.

1977   Wilkins retires as secretary of the NAACP after forty-six years of service.

1981   Roy Wilkins dies on September 8.

Sources

CHAPTER ONE: From Poverty to Prosperity

p. 10, "Everyone around us . . ." Roy Wilkins with Tom Mathews, *Standing Fast: The Autobiography of Roy Wilkins* (New York: The Viking Press, 1982), 30.

p. 11-12, "No one can . . ." Ibid.

p. 14, "Nigger, get out . . ." Ibid., 16.

p. 14, "My grandfather had . . ." Roger Wilkins, "What Really Matters Is That You Keep Up the Struggle: interview with Roger Wilkins," Voices of Civil Rights, http://www.voicesofcivilrights.org/civil3_2004_04_rw.html, (accessed November 20, 2004).

p. 14, "ran north . . ." Ibid.

p. 16, "I have the . . ." Wilkins, *Standing Fast,* 16.

p. 19, "Education may be . . ." Ibid., 9.

p. 19, "the world was . . ." Ibid., 23.

CHAPTER TWO: Birth of the NAACP

p. 21, "Cast down your . . ." Booker T. Washington, "Booker T. Washington Delivers the 1895 Atlanta Compromise Speech," History Matters, http://historymatters.gmu.edu/d/39/, (accessed November 12, 2004).

p. 21, "it is in the South . . ." Ibid.

p. 24, "The Negro race . . ." Francis L. Broderick and August Meier, *Negro Protest Thought in the Twentieth Century* (Indianapolis: The Bobbs-Merrill Company, Inc., 1965), 41.

p. 30, "an effaceable stain . . ." "The Lynchings," Duluth Lynchings Online Resource, http://collections.mnhs.org/duluthlynchings/html/lynchings.htm, (accessed September 30, 2004).

p. 30, "sick, scared and . . ." Wilkins, *Standing Fast,* 44.

p. 30-31, "For the first time . . ." Ibid., 44

CHAPTER THREE: Newspaper Crusader

p. 38, "Du Bois acknowledges . . ." Wilkins, *Standing Fast,* 52.

p. 40, "Look around you . . ." Ibid., 54.

CHAPTER FOUR: Return to the South

p. 44, "She eyed me frostily . . ." Wilkins, *Standing Fast,* 60.

p. 48, "The color line . . ." Ibid., 70.

p. 50, "quite a hullabaloo . . ." Sheila Tully Boyle and Andrew Bunie, *Paul Robeson: The Years of Promise and Achievement* (Amherst: University of Massachusetts Press, 2001), 182.

p. 51, "Since [Robeson] was advertised . . ." Ibid.

p. 51, "God grant that . . ." Ibid., 183.

CHAPTER FIVE: Time for Change

p. 57, "Nothing contributes so . . ." Kenneth Robert Janken, *White: The Biography of Walter White, Mr. NAACP* (New York: The New Press, 2001), 53.

p. 59, "In a very . . ." Ibid., 16.

p. 60, "some good comes . . ." Wilkins, *Standing Fast,* 91.

p. 60, "We want to . . ." Janken, *White,* 137.

p. 60, "a source of . . ." David Levering Lewis, *W.E.B. Du Bois,* vol. 2, *The Fight for Equality and the American Century* (New York: Henry Holt and Company, 2000), 251.

p. 61, "If I should . . ." Wilkins, *Standing Fast,* 91.

p. 62, "It all comes . . ." Ibid., 92.

p. 63, "a political cloud . . ." Janken, *White,* 142.

p. 64, "Dr. Du Bois went out . . ." Marvel Cooke, interview by Kathleen Currie, "Marvel Cooke: Interview No. 3 (pp. 51-65)" Washington Press Club Foundation, http://npc.press.org/wpforal/cook3.htm, (accessed November 17, 2004).

p. 64, "share whole-heartedly the . . ." Lewis, *W.E.B. Du Bois,* 279.

p. 64-65, "reasonable and not . . ." Ibid., 280.

p. 67, "couldn't understand what . . ." Wilkins, *Standing Fast,* 99.

p. 70, "You may say . . ." Ibid., 105.

CHAPTER SIX: A New Career

p. 77, "trying to put . . ." Raymond Wolters, *Du Bois and His Rivals* (Columbia: University of Missouri Press, 2002), 213.

p. 77, "You see . . ." Ibid., 212.

p. 78-79, "In a mess . . ." Roy Wilkins, "The Bonuseers Ban Jim Crow," in *A Documentary History of the Negro People in the United States: 1910-1932,* ed. Herbert Aptheker, (New York: Carol Publishing Group, 1973) 737.

p. 79, "The [marchers] proved . . ." Ibid., 738.

p. 84, "the ignorance and . . ." Janken, *White,* 150.

CHAPTER SEVEN: Jim Crow Goes to War

p. 91, "the Association seems . . ." Janken, *White,* 175.

p. 91, "had neither the . . ." Lewis, *W.E.B. Du Bois,* 336.

p. 92, "a liar and . . ." Ibid., 337.

p. 92, "It is impossible . . ." Ibid.

p. 92, "It must be . . ." Ibid., 338.

p. 93, "Dr. Du Bois's sudden . . ." Wilkins, *Standing Fast,* 154.

p. 97, "no single issue . . ." Lewis, *W.E.B. Du Bois,* 465.

p. 100, "Walter couldn't have . . ." Wilkins, *Standing Fast,* 180.

p. 100-101, "Mr. President, we . . . Mr. President," Jervis Anderson, *A. Philip Randolph: A Biographical Portrait,* (New York: Harcourt Brace Jovanovich, Inc., 1972), 257.

p. 101, "[T]here shall be . . ." Daniel S. Davis, *Mr. Black Labor: The Story of A. Philip Randolph, Father of the Civil Rights Movement* (New York: E.P. Dutton & Co., Inc., 1972), 109.

p. 101-102, "To this day . . ." Wilkins, *Standing Fast,* 180.

p. 102, "traditional NAACP attitude . . ." Janken, *White,* 258.

p. 103, "some people [could believe] . . ." Ibid., 259.

CHAPTER EIGHT: The Fight Becomes Clear

p. 108, "Tokyo and Berlin . . ." Janken, *White,* 274.

p. 109, "Walter was as . . ." Wilkins, *Standing Fast,* 183.

p. 110, "Jews were beaten . . ." Ibid., 184.

p. 110, "criminal and unforgivable," Janken, *White,* 276.

p. 112, "We might have . . ." Wilkins, *Standing Fast,* 186.

p. 116, "loaded [the NAACP] . . ." Janken, *White,* 316.

CHAPTER NINE: The Top Job

p. 118, "broke the ground . . ." Wilkins, *Standing Fast,* 196.

p. 120, "there shall be . . ." Davis, *Mr. Black Labor,* 130.

p. 121, "the mood among . . ." Anderson, *A. Philip Randolph*, 276.

p. 122, "There is no . . ." Wilkins, *Standing Fast,* 202.

p. 123, "unwittingly placed in . . ." Janken, *White,* 339.

p. 125, "One aspect of . . ." Ibid., 352.

p. 128, "The only emotion . . ." Wilkins, *Standing Fast,* 213.

p. 129, "Who but Walter . . ." Ibid., 220.

p. 130, "And we are . . ." Roberta Hughes White, *The Birth of the Montgomery Bus Boycott* (Southfield, MI: Charro Press Inc., 1991), 84.

p. 130, "We are quite . . ." Taylor Branch, *Parting the Waters: America in the King Years: 1954-63* (New York: Simon and Schuster, 1988), 186.

CHAPTER TEN: Not Backing Down

p. 136, "incomparably the most . . ." Branch, *Parting the Waters,* 221.

p. 137, "How silly can . . ." Ibid.

p. 137, "If you are . . ." Ibid.

p. 138, "The manicured hands . . ." Roy Wilkins, ed. Sondra Kathryn Wilson, *In Search of Democracy: The NAACP Writings of James Weldon Johnson, Walter White and Roy Wilkins (1920-1977)* (New York: Oxford University Press, 1999), 371.

p. 139, "Now begins the . . ." Branch, *Parting the Waters,* 224.

p. 139, "What baloney," Wilkins, *Standing Fast,* 252.

p. 145, "living petition for . . ." Wilkins, *In Search of Democracy,* 408.

p. 147, "Contrary to the . . ." Ibid., 407.

p. 150, "at the dawn . . ." Branch, *Parting the Waters,* 878.

p. 150, "Just by your . . ." Ibid., 410.

p. 150, "Of all the . . ." Robert Dallek, *Flawed Giant: Lyndon Johnson and His Times: 1961-1973* (New York: Oxford University Press, 1998), 26.

CHAPTER ELEVEN: Promises Kept

p. 151, "[no] eulogy could . . ." Dallek, *Flawed Giant,* 60.

p. 152, "I want that . . ." Wilkins, *Standing Fast,* 296.

p. 153, "They can filibuster . . ." Dallek, *Flawed Giant,* 117.

p. 153, "They say I'm . . ." Ibid., 118.

p. 154, "violent and futile . . ." Taylor Branch, *Pillar of Fire: America in the King Years: 1963-65* (New York: Simon and Schuster, 1998), 423.

p. 154-155, "Negro trouble . . . broad curtailment," Ibid., 424.

p. 155, "have sold themselves . . ." Ibid.

p. 155, "a usurpation of . . ." Ibid., 357.

p. 155, "I came away . . ." Wilkins, *Standing Fast,* 311.

p. 158, "Well, I guess . . ." David Halberstam, *The Children* (New York: Random House, 1998), 450.

p. 159, "there was no . . ." Stokely Carmichael, with Ekwueme Michael Thelwell, *Ready for Revolution: The Life and Struggles of Stokely Carmichael (Kwame Ture)* (New York: Scribner, 2003), 499.

p. 160, "I couldn't help . . ." Ibid.

p. 160, "Times change; the . . ." Wilkins, *Standing Fast,* 53.

p. 163, "civil rights movement . . ." Ibid., 341.

p. 163, "A racial minority . . ." Ibid., 436.

Bibliography

Anderson, Jervis. *A. Philip Randolph: A Biographical Portrait.* New York: Harcourt Brace Jovanovich, Inc., 1972.

Boyle, Sheila Tully and Andrew Bunie. *Paul Robeson: The Years of Promise and Achievement.* Amherst: University of Massachusetts Press, 2001.

Branch, Taylor. *Parting the Waters: America in the King Years: 1954-63.* New York: Simon and Schuster, 1988.

———. *Pillar of Fire: America in the King Years: 1963-65.* New York: Simon and Schuster, 1998.

Broderick, Francis L. and August Meier. *Negro Protest Thought in the Twentieth Century.* Indianapolis: The Bobbs-Merrill Company, Inc., 1965.

Carmichael, Stokely with Ekwueme Michael Thelwell. *Ready for Revolution: The Life and Struggles of Stokely Carmichael (Kwame Ture).* New York: Scribner, 2003.

Cooke, Marvel. "Marvel Cooke: Interview No. 3 (pp. 51-65)" by Kathleen Currie. Washington Press Club Foundation, http://npc.press.org/ wpforal/cook3.htm, (accessed November 17, 2004).

Dallek, Robert. *Flawed Giant: Lyndon Johnson and His Times: 1961-1973.* New York: Oxford University Press, 1998.

Davis, Daniel S. *Mr. Black Labor: The Story of A. Philip Randolph, Father of the Civil Rights Movement.* New York: E.P. Dutton & Co., Inc., 1972.

Halberstam, David. *The Children*. New York: Random House, 1998.

Janken, Kenneth Robert. *White: The Biography of Walter White, Mr. NAACP*. New York: The New Press, 2001.

Lewis, David Levering. *The Fight for Equality and the American Century,* Vol. 2 of *W.E.B. Du Bois.* New York: Henry Holt and Company, 2000.

"The Lynchings." Duluth Lynchings Online Resource, http://collections.mnhs.org/duluthlynchings/html/lynchings.htm, (accessed September 30, 2004).

Washington, Booker T. "Booker T. Washington Delivers the 1895 Atlanta Compromise Speech." History Matters, http://historymatters.gmu.edu/d/39/, (accessed November 12, 2004).

White, Roberta Hughes. *The Birth of the Montgomery Bus Boycott*. Southfield, MI: Charro Press Inc., 1991.

Wilkins, Roger. "What Really Matters Is That You Keep Up the Struggle: interview with Roger Wilkins." Voices of Civil Rights. http://www.voicesofcivilrights.org/civil3_2004_04_rw.html, (accessed November 20, 2004).

Wilkins, Roy. "The Bonuseers Ban Jim Crow," in *A Documentary History of the Negro People in the United States: 1910-1932,* ed. Herbert Aptheker. New York: Carol Publishing Group, 1973.

———— with Tom Mathews. *Standing Fast: The Autobiography of Roy Wilkins.* New York: The Viking Press, 1982.

———— in *In Search of Democracy: The NAACP Writings of James Weldon Johnson, Walter White and Roy Wilkins (1920-1977),* ed. Sondra Kathryn Wilson. New York: Oxford University Press, 1999.

Wolters, Raymond. *Du Bois and His Rivals*. Columbia: University of Missouri Press, 2002.

Web sites

http://www.core-online.org/
The official site of the Congress of Racial Equality.

http://www.tsum.edu/museum/
The Troy State University Montgomery Rosa Parks Library and Museum.

http://www.cr.nps.gov/nr/travel/civilrights/
A site maintained by the National Parks Service offering information about historic sites related to the civil rights movement.

http://www.usccr.gov/
The online home of the United States Commission on Civil Rights.

http://www.civilrights.org/
The home page of the Civil Rights Coalition.

http://www.civilrightsmuseum.org/
The online home of the National Civil Rights Museum, located in the former Lorraine Motel, where Martin Luther King Jr. was shot.

http://www.naacp.org/
The home page of the NAACP.

Index